White Lighter Full of Phoenix Fire

Robert T. West

First paperback edition January 2021
ISBN #978-0-578-77218-9

Interior Book design by Tilly McGill of Midnight Oil Design

Cover format and Back Cover Art by Tilly McGill of Midnight Oil Design

Front Cover art by Jesse Martin @jesse_martin

Table of Contents

Acknowledgments,

I wrote this one for me, and me alone. But you're reading it now so it must be for you too.

-RTW

BROTHERHOOD & BOYHOOD
(Each Excuses)

"A wasted youth is better by far than a wise and productive old age." – Meatloaf

Everything I Am

-It's all packed up again-

-three bags to throw on my back and turn me to mincemeat-

-the weight applied is not for strength-

-only to shred my youth and cartilage between my very bones-

-laid upon my back, I know, I know to not hold onto to hopes of an unknown home-

-instead, I cling to what is known-

-when I bag up all I have, I make room for Everything I am-

Formicidae

Ants creep up cerebral stalks in search of whatever serotonin I have left.

Hungry pinchers carry it off to another garrison workday.

Soon enough, the weight sinks back, but it's nothing, leave weeks and weekend drinks can't uplift?

Desperation settles stale and blank-faced into a groove of daily repetitions.

Uniforms once proudly worn, twist in my inner vision. Little camo boxes and blotches shift into grayscale until I'm left buttoning up a prisoner's regalia each morning.

Guilt and suspicion plague every step until I've fashioned my ball and chain.

I thought they'd teach me discipline, maybe find pride in who I am. All I've learned is how to make my lies cleverer and a skewed view of my "better's."

So, fingers fumble buttons and press pins, all while the ants come marching again. Single file as if to hide their numbers, but each microscopic footfall reverberates a sensation, a sane man might mistake for numbness.

As the crawling reaches a zenith, my reflection mocks all that I would try to be.

Watching it sneer back at me, I long for a day when my hair touches my shoulder blades, and I rip these sleeves free like a beatnik rocker's fever dream.

Alas, for now, the ants are marching, and I'll keep pace.

High Mileage

A red light burns behind my eyes in a visage of an
ethereal engine light.

It tells me next to nothing. Only that trouble is ahead.

But no shop exists for an intangible self, and my search for
mechanics is nil.

Who is even qualified?

A silent god?

A mirror?

Her?

And how many more miles till I'm only good for parts?

<u>Are we the children</u> of him on high?

-or-

Coalesced stardust pulled from the sky?

Are we Legends to be?

-or-

Pests to ancient trees?

Are we, our Father's whores and our mother's
bastards or do I have that one
backwards?

Are we act or are we intent?

Discover

For now, we are not fit.

As the

Crow flies I can see the wound

from miles away.

I smell the blood and rush eagle-eyed and hungry for any pain that isn't mine.

I'll feat on yours while I pack my wounds with apathy.

Center of His-story

What becomes of a boy raising himself through Hero's stories?

From Lee to Doyle, he'd never believe that he'd become his own foil.

This life came with no cape draped over shoulders to keep his conscience warm and out of sight, but now he'll stand with prying eyes abound, yet it isn't the attention he fears.

Each and every, they offer up a single apathetic blink and turn to the next startling thing. This lets him know he is the only one surprised by his own villainy.

What a tale this turned out to be.

Debrief

When did it change?

The talk used to be about life, country, and liberty.

Now it's all commerce and prosperity.

They've made hands for war then shied away. Giving
only tight leashes to choke the freedoms we don't
know why we gave so cheaply,

Prattle on, prattle on,

But this war won't come.

Not how we want, all flags and guns.

It's lost I tell you,

It's sold like a whore,

Learn instead to fight your own wars.

Generations I've been
little brother and big brother with no blood in
between,

Instead,

I've shared advice, insights, lessons, and spite,

I've shown care, lent an ear, I've stolen, and lied.

But I can't save you, I can't keep you alive,

Self-aide my brother. Don't let us both die.

WE KNEEL AT THE ALTER
OF
  VIOLENCE

ONLY TO SMIRK WHEN
   PRAYERS MEET
   SILENCE.

Give me a junkyard,

Not a pedigree exists for a mutt like me.

Not a home has been known as far as I see.

They'll throw beds in a kennel but this tramps gotta roam.

Not a home has been known as far as I see.

No lady in a back alley making an honest man of me.

Not a home has been known as far as I see.

Messy hair and chipped teeth tell you I'm not the dream you'd thought I'd be.

Not a home has been known as far as I see.

Hippocratic hypocrite

An oath so empty, it's neither broken nor fulfilled.
What kind of hope is it to only be tested when your
brother is killed?

I should thank any empty god.

They kept my soul unchecked and unstained by this
covenant.

This Bloodline is deep.

This Bloodline is old.

This Bloodline is stagnant.

This Bloodline is cold.

Some have made money.

Some have made homes.

I am not some,

Here poor on these

roads.

So walking, I know.

I know in my soul,

I am more than,

This Flesh,

This Blood,

These Bones.

Childish Games

Bloody knuckles on the playground turn to more than just games.

Soon, it's brawls outside when the whiskey takes hold.

Back alleys to parking lots, and laughing like fiends when we're running from the cops.

It's been so long since they slapped irons on my wrists.

I've just gotta wonder if I'm made for this.

<u>Hunting for Balance</u> I feel like a poor man pinching
pennies.
Peace today seems just out of reach.
Still, I find my feet marching to the beat.

Sluggish, dragging, I can't keep in step.

But the cadence promises a place I ain't been yet.

What's left after the melancholy wears thin?

If you sift the boredom long enough, more will surface.

I found myself praying without an ounce of faith.

The only fuel I can spark is righteous self-hate.

But maybe that'll get the message through.

Maybe that'll pay the dues of a prodigal son that are long past due.

Shitbag Breed

Black Patch boy, born a rebel from the jump.

He's a been a fan of bloody knuckles from a young age.

Was made that way through borrowed rage he'd kept long past due.

He'll run with that contentious streak that recruit depots and a hundred SNCO's couldn't beat.

They talk career's not callings, so he's hung up the phone.

His minutes are up, and he hasn't found a home.

Pranayama

Inhale-

Let the Smoke bring ease,

Inhale

Make the diagram flex,

Inhale

Let the rebreather work,

Exhale

Let the trigger squeeze,

Exhale

Make the mind at peace,

Exhale

Make anger flow free,

_-

Breath/Live/ Repeat

Breath/Live/Repeat

Tantrums,

Tantrums Do

they age well?

Recall, recall,

Pull them from the shelves.

Stale, Stale

But I eat it still.

Spores, Spores,

They grow thick and I grow ill.

Story time

It's nothing much.

Just a bunch of kids telling other people's war stories.

We all hope if we keep feeding it months and years,
this one-armed bandit will give us stories all our own.

Patrol

Sun had snuck its way through Ernest's window. Well, not that Ernest could claim the window. The two feet by four feet pane of dusty glass was no more his than the blanket he pulled over his head. While it was warm and blocked out the sun, a faint musty smell clung to it at all times and was impossible to ignore when it covered his face. He toyed with the idea of getting up and facing the day when a boot made the decision for him.

"Come on, suns already up, you know what it means!" came the caterwaul of a pubescent drawl. The speaker, Garth, tried his best to keep the tone low and commanding, but a squeaking crack snuck in, that he tried to hide behind a cough while he strutted around the exposed bricks that corralled them. "Come on! We've got work!" the artificial depth of voice was back just like that.

Ernest tossed the smelly blanket and swung his socked feet off of the bedroll he had been resting on last night. Around him, he heard the rustling of his team, stirring themselves with the help of their leader's words. He rushed to stuff his socked feet in the cracked black leather of the boots, sitting neatly beside each other toes outboard.

"What the fuck are you doing?" Garth growled. Ernest looked up from his task at the young boy, who had seemingly apparated before him. He was admittedly confused at what infraction he might have committed and still, in a waking stupor. Garth was looking down on him. He was a head taller than any of their little group. He stood like a thin bean pole in his faded jeans, bloused over brown leather work boots that had extreme care taken to them. His plain brown crew neck shirt was tucked in, held in place by a frayed web belt that held up a leather holster and a sheath. Each was a beautiful blonde leather with some flowery patterns tooled across their surfaces. On his right hip, the holster held a heavy blued steel revolver that seemed to rest comically in Garth's bony hands anytime he produced it. On the right was a stag handled bowie knife. Sitting atop this character was a vulpine face with a mop of brown hair lead by dark animal eyes that had been dulled by overwhelming instinct that had become Garth's very being.

Ernest spoke.

"Putting on my boots, we've gotta…" he was interrupted by a quick pop to the back of his crew cut head that rocked him forward and made him flinch instinctually.

"No, shit? With yesterday's socks still on?" Garth asked

Ernest blinked in response and looked down at the grey and black boot socks that had been on his feet all night.

"Your fucking feet are gonna rot off if you keep doing stupid shit like that. Now change them and hurry up; we don't have all morning." And with that, Garth strode away to inspect the other two team members while Ernest busied himself with changing socks and gathering everything.

The other two were busy with the same.

James, a darker-skinned boy, while older than Ernest, surely wasn't a teenager like Garth. He was bald and carried a drooping face that Ernest had seen brighten only a handful of times and only from fear or excitement. He, too, was skinny, as they all were, but not boasting any height made him as tall as Ernest but without much hope for any more growth spurts.

He was ahead of the others in waking and preparations, already tightening the straps of an olive drab aluminum frame pack. Ernest didn't envy that pack; sure, it had a bedroll and a tin canteen strapped to the outside as they all did, but the insides swelled. It was pregnant with contents, both heavy and dour. Little metal spheres that rolled against each other as the pack settled on his back. Grenades. Ernest never knew why the four of them needed so many grenades, but no one a higher rank than Garth had ever bothered him with his requests, and he assured them that they'd come in handy when they "got into it.".

Garth was the only one who'd "gotten into it" out of their team. Several times, when Garth deemed it safe enough to speak during night encampments, he'd show the scar that ran up his back, across the nape of his neck to just behind his ear. It was a burn that wrinkled and marred the skin in a sweeping crescent that looked as though it might close its maw around his bony left shoulder blade.

At the time, Garth had been just a simple footboy like Ernest and the others, and his team was clearing out a street with a menagerie of empty stores lining its sidewalks. Back then, five or six teams might work in tandem when they expected trouble, and this had been one of those days. While Garth and his team were moving down the street, a machine gun opened up. "fully auto," Garth would say with a menacing smile every time he told the story. It had turned a dozen or so footboys into still and shredded corpses in moments.
Ernest shuddered at the thought, he'd never came across anything like that with his time in the militia.

"All right, time to step!" Garth's voice shook him from the macabre daydream.

Garth was fastening a green loadbearing vest about himself. Its straps lined with pockets and pouches full of who knew what. But along its hip belt were brass bullets fat and gleaming ready to be fed into his revolver's cylinders prepared to slaughter some faceless enemy and a blocky green radio handset with a reedlike antenna screwed into it's top.

Ernest fought to make time, throwing his own aluminum frame pack onto his shoulders and tightening down its straps, and snatching up a Kalashnikov with a skeletal folding buttstock of stamped metal and a curving magazine its two-point sling fit snugly over his torso.

As he crossed the room, he almost bumped against his final teammate: Julius, a light-skinned boy, roughly the same age as Ernest with unkempt dark hair, a smattering of freckles, and always chapped lips that he was sequentially licking with no waking breaks. Across his torso was a slim magazine-fed rifle that, according to Garth, was not as nice as Ernest's.

The quartet took their guns, knives, and little bombs down the stairs found just outside the door of the room they'd made refuge in that night.

"What are we even doing?" Julius muttered. Sleep was heavy in his voice. As the team's newest member, Julius had two night-watch shifts where James and Ernest had only one, and it must have left him tired.

Garth grunted and tapped the radio with an open palm.

"I got word from higher. We patrol down from the square to the outskirts of downtown. They're gonna push

45

some troopers down the interstate and want us to set up a watch over the bridge to make sure the way is clear."

Ernest wasn't sure who higher was. Maybe they were the ones that had shown up and told his parents they needed to give up their son to the cause. Those two were full-blown teenagers; one of them might even be twenty. And they carried very lovely guns, even nicer than Garth's. Ernest was so happy he'd been able to become a footboy; he didn't have to work in the factories or fill crates with ammunition, parts, or rations anymore. He'd seen many young boys die from the machines or get sick. Now he knew, when he died, people would remember him.

"We gonna get to see the troopers?" Julius followed up as they stepped into the street. The building they were exiting was, at one point, a governmental one from what Ernest understood, which meant people had made decisions there. He supposed it was like how garth made decisions. When those decisions were made, other people agreed and followed through with them.

Ernest didn't know why people would need a building because Garth made the decisions anywhere, he needed to. But maybe that's why people stopped using them.

Garth shrugged at them and fished in his pocket for the cigarettes he kept in the pouch up near his chest.

"We may, may not, just keep fucking walking." He said, feeding his lips a slim white stick that always made him look a little older to Ernest. He'd be a trooper one day, Ernest was sure. Another year of patrols like this and Garth would be marching out to faraway lands to send food and other things grown-ups need back home to people like Ernest's parents. He couldn't remember much about them, but he thought it was funny because he remembered the cots they'd slept on were better than his bedroll. They had chickens in their backyard and a small garden as well, so Ernest wasn't sure what else grown-ups needed.

The four of them walked down the road in a little diamond shape with Ernest upfront. This was a place of pride for him; he'd be the first one to see and call out any dangers to the rest of his team. Even though all he saw now was a street lined with a layer of dust that would pick up in little tornadoes when the wind picked up, all along the side of the road that they stepped down where old storefronts. Each of them appeared the same all square and ubiquitous. They only seemed to differ with the presentation of their individual fates. Most were empty and broken in. long ago abandoned by anyone but the squatters that everyone had detested. A few had, for some unknown reason, become the receptacle of mountains of trash and rubbish that covered the storefronts as if great winds had piled them up to clear the way for the little dust tornadoes it loved to make. The minority of these buildings were freshly boarded up—a sign of change. Just last summer, vendors were in there selling all manner of things.

Ernest could remember them. A man who would work on scooters, bikes, and small motored vehicles, a woman and her husband who sold the footboys meats at a discounted price, a man who repaired watches, and another fixed shoes, two or three odd shops sold random general goods.

But most had left with the winter. And when came spring, the militia started moving footboys, and now troopers around and through the town drove the others away.

"Soldiers don't pay for things." Garth had explained once when they'd been on patrol and seen a group of older footboys and a few troopers walking through the shops taking what they want without trading or paying for what they took.

"We do more than them. We do things they can't and things they just won't," he'd continued. While they both had been standing watching, Ernest hadn't asked Garth for any advice. It was strange to him.

"It's alright," Garth had said softly before continuing to whatever else they had to patrol that day.

But now, the streets weren't busy. No vendors and no soldiers were taking what they should. Only trash, dust, and dead shrubs were making homes between empty buildings.

After a few more minutes of the silent procession, they had exited the square leaving the dilapidated shops behind as the relatively tight and orderly layout of the town square kept growing farther and farther apart.

Now a smattering of business and residences all in states of similar disuse stood as stoic onlookers to the Footboys parade. These crumbling monuments to domestic life were accompanied only by sickly trees and skeletal shrubbery shooting up from yellow grass that meshed well with the patina overtone of the dusty surroundings.

Ernest's eyes flickered between all these looming giants. Knowing that behind anyone might be the enemy militia or senseless bandits he'd heard so much about. With every step, he felt a growing anxiety buzz at the back of his head. Phantom eyes that may or may not even exist hunted him from every blind spot. Rather than this, grow into fidgeting nervousness or become a gnawing neurotic fear eventually, it slowly plateaued into banality. It became a steady, mindful awareness that would pull him back to the present when his mind began to wander into the territory of daydreams.

"Ern, you see that?" he heard James's voice mutter in a low tone over his right shoulder. His eyes searched for a frightful second until his gaze fixed on a dark figure some 200 meters ahead on the road.

With embarrassment flushing up to his neck, he gave a curt nod as if entirely untroubled by the approaching figure. He realized maybe he still wasn't as mindful as he thought he was.

He raised a hand signal to indicate the little group to a halt.

"Spread out," Garth ordered. "Jul, J, get to either side of the road Ern you stick by me."

The boys obeyed their leader in silence. Ern straightened his back,
letting pride swell in his bird chest at his position at his leader's side while facing this threat.

Only, after a few minutes passed, the threat grew less threatening with its nearness.

What had begun as a slinking figure in the distance quickly shifted. It was a slim woman with dark lank hair framing an emaciated face glazed over with the same grim he saw on the faces of his fellows. A loose brown dress and tan jacket hung limply off her unsubstantial frame. It was fastened in the middle by either a belt or a span of rope acting like one. It swayed with her steps and fluttered with the stale breeze. Pulled behind her was a sizeable wagon piled high with various bags and what appeared to be scrap metal cans and trinkets.

"All right, Ern," Garth spoke with a hint of satisfaction buoying each word. "It looks like some kind of squatter or scavenger. She prolly ain't one of our citizens, so we're gonna search her stuff. You just stand by and keep looking tough, so she knows not to fuck with us."

Ern tightened his grip on the rifle and brought the buttstock closer to his shoulder, thinking of the few times he'd gotten to shoot it. The way it had bit and dug into his shoulder and how loud it had been. The ex-trooper in charge of showing them had yelled at him for how shaky his hands had been after firing. He nodded to Garth; his hand yanked the charging handle on the side of the rifle. He steeled himself in case the shakes came back. Meanwhile, Garth stood beside him with a sly little grin and a hand lazily cupping the curved grip of his pistol.

The woman came within 20meters of them before garth yelled out. He did a good job of not letting his voice crack this time.

"Close enough now. Go ahead and step away from the wagon and keep your hands at your side, just doing an inspection." The woman scoffed but complied, taking five sizable steps away from her wagon and standing still as the near leafless trees around them. While approaching the wagon with an easy swagger, Garth motioned with a thrust of his chin towards the woman, and Ernest raised his rifle slightly in her direction, giving the passive threat of violence if she moved wrong.

"Well, I don't have much. Some other bandits beat you to it a day or two back." She said. Her voice carried apathetic spite that Ernest had only heard from adults.

Garth had barely started rooting through the woman's pile of rubbish when this comment made him spin on his heels.

"What the fuck did you say to me bitch?" it came out peaked by the kind of adolescent tenor that shines through when a kid gets heated.

"I'm just saying there ain't much for y'all to go stealing." She said with a shrug.

"Stealing? I'm a Foot team leader for the Convent's militia. Not a damn bandit, you dusty cunt!" She let out a sigh.

"Sure, kid. Whatever. How much longer do you need?" Ernest was concerned he'd never seen someone be this flippant with Garth before. He wouldn't like it.

Sure enough, with a twisted-up face, he dropped his right hand to his pistol again and with the left, he pointed to the ground.

"Get on your fucking face." He growled, and she complied slowly, kneeling with tenderness as if the act caused her pain.

Once she was lying prostrate, he looked to Ernest.

"Search her, make sure she ain't hiding anything."

Ernest stepped towards her tentatively, slinging his rifle to the side.

As he knelt over her, he got a closer look at her face. It was impossible to ignore the way she stared. Her dark, almond-shaped eyes looked large and bug like on her gaunt face. Some of what he'd thought to be grime and dirt from the road turned out to be a mix of scabs and old scars that clung to her face as lichen clings to the trunks of trees. Her lips themselves reminded him of the roads, colorless and cracked parallel lines that pated ever so slightly as she breathed a rattling breath out it.

His hands patted her form, awkward and unsure exactly of what to do. He was instantly squeamish. She felt like a cold bag of kindling sticks one might use to feed a new fire rather than a human body. But out of these bony protrusions, Ernest did feel something that stirred his heart to a faster beat. A curved shape in the small of her back just under the coat. His hand rested on it for a moment, and she seemed to stir uneasily under him. He was fairly sure of what it was and, despite himself, feared what might come next.

His eyes flicked to Garth, who was bent over the mound of items in her wagon. No point in asking what to do that would only waste time. He pulled up the hem of the coat to show the small of her back, and sure enough, there *It* was.

Tucked into the rope-belt around her waist, was a small rusty revolver with a beat-up chestnut handle.

His small hand shot out and pulled it free from its hiding place.

"Hey, no, I need that. It's not safe on the road!" she protested, rolling onto her side. For a moment, he thought she might reach out to snatch the weapon back, and he scrambled back an arm's length away.

"Well, well. That's two strikes, lady." Garth said. Ernest stood and looked over to him.

He held a string tied to what looked to be the limp form of a dead animal with long matted off-white fur—a dead cat.

"You wouldn't happen to be one of the Convents hunters, would yah? Killin animals on convent territory ain't legal without it," he asked, leering.

"No, what? I found that this morning! It's just roadkill." Her nonchalant monotone had given way to a pleading tone of concern.

"Oh, of course, you did." Garth said with mocking reassurance, "Well, since you ain't no hunter, and you're packing a gun, you must be a soldier, right? Which troop are you with?" She began a frantic stream of stammering that Ernest couldn't follow. It was hard for him to follow any of what was unfolding, really.

"Just shut up bitch!" Garth barked, silencing her but not soothing her fidgeting restlessness. "You. Hand me that!" he said to Ernest with an outstretched hand.

Ernest complied, handing it grip first over to his team leader.

Garth had his jaw clenched in quiet rage as he examined. It was a pitiful thing compared to his. A shorter barrel, smaller frame, and the chrome was long tarnished and covered in rust around it's cracked and beaten grip bits of stained white tape seemed to help hold it together. He popped the cylinder open and squinted into it.

"Hmmph…" he said with a little smirk starting to spread, "two little bullets. Ain't much."

He snapped the cylinder closed.

"But enough to kill my teammate and me. That's enough for me." He let the statement hang in the air until it was cemented as a threat.

"Please, uh sir, I'll turn around, keep the cat. Take anything you want, just let me keep the…" and she reached up and was met with a swift boot to the forehead. That connected with a jarring *wack* that made Ernest flinch inadvertently and rocked her head back.

"Now, don't be making any moves bitch. You're detained." His smile was a sinister grin. He shot a look over at Ernest, observed him for a moment, then adopted a look of mild bewilderment. Meanwhile, the woman on the ground kept blabbering on panic pouring from her throat.

"Come on, come on… I know. You're a young guy. I bet you haven't had your dick sucked too many times?" Garth's gaze shot back down to the woman on the ground, who now had a trickle of blood flowing freely down her face from the impact of his bootheel. His face took on an appearance that

Ernest was so unfamiliar with his leader that he could barely identify it. But yes, sure enough, that was a red-faced embarrassment.

"Yeah, it'll be good. You'll love it hell do whatever you want we can have some fun. Come on, come on! Wouldn't that be better?" she was pleading on hands and knees, looking up at garth, whose rage was returning.

Her vulgar offers kept going for another moment before Garth very coldly spoke.

"Shut your whore mouth." He said before turning to Ernest and speaking matter-of-factly.

"You ain't killed anyone yet, have you?"

Ern was still frozen in confusion, but now a cold sweat broke out on his back.

"Well?" this time, Garth had brought some steel back to his voice.

Ernest shook his head. Garth's grin spread warmly this time as he raised the confiscated revolver towards Ernest. Handle first just as it had been handed to him.

"Go ahead, pop your cherry boy." The statement was so disturbingly excited and inviting. Slowly Ernest reached out and gripped the small pistol in his hand, registered it with a kind of dull confusion before leveling it at the woman on the ground.

Her eyes were even more prominent than before. Now stretched to near inhumane width with fear. She croaked out one final plea.

"Please."

Ernest felt a flood of confusion. It seemed like it should be so easy to squeeze the trigger. So why hadn't he yet?

He felt frozen in time, frozen with his eyes looking over the barrel at the ghoulish face of the supposedly foreign woman.

It was so easy, just squeeze. Why wouldn't he just squeeze?

Then a jarring cannon blast rocked the patch of road that set the scene. Usually, such a thing would force Ernest to cringe, but the scene in front of him transfixed him. His eyes were forced to stay open by the grotesque fascination brought on by the woman's head, the front left portion, right below her hairline, erupting in a spray of a

55

deep crimson. What was once the top of her head was now a deflated and obtuse mess with sickeningly pink flaps of skin flapping as she fell forward.

The air was still, save the slowly retreating echo and the uncanny twitches of the woman's body. It was if she was pretending to be cold and shivering but taken to an uncanny hideous degree of overacting. In the air was the metal of lifeblood and an acrid burning of gun smoke.

There was no denying what happened. Ernest's gun hand fell

defeated and shaking to his side. He didn't want to look, but just like how he couldn't avoid watching the woman's head split, he couldn't help but turn his gaze to Garth.

He stood with his face made placid by grim satisfaction. One long skinny arm outstretched like a scythe-wielding reaper. But in his knuckles, he gripped his long-barreled black revolver. Garth replaced it into its holster's smooth leather, and he threw a quick look of dismissive annoyance at Ernest, who still clutched his gun with shaking white knuckles.

Damn it, why wouldn't he stop shaking.

The rest of the scene whizzed by numbly. It was filled with Garth's vague mutterings on the green radio relaying some version of the incident to some faceless person on the other side. Then they went about "investigating" the woman's belongings.

It went in a pecking order.

Naturally, with Garth first. Who found some thick mirrored glasses sporting neat silver frames?

"Bitch would've got a pretty penny for these, huh?" he asked with a consensus of "Damn straight!" by the other two.

James was next. He found a broken watch with one leather strap missing that looked as though it might be possible to repair.

Next was Ernest, who, when he moved to rummage, was stopped by Garth.

"Nuh, uh Ern. You've got the biggest prize already. Just make sure you pull the damn trigger next time." At first, Ernest's daze made the words a riddle. Then he remembered the new gun tucked into his waistband. He wasn't sure he wanted it. But he was sure he didn't feel like rummaging again.

Finally, it was Julius. He mostly just found cause to complain that everything in the wagon was trash before he found a big bent coin with a bearded figure. Jules was damned sure it was worth something.

"That's just a hunk of junk. It ain't even real monies. They call them novelties, Jules." Garth tried to warn him to no avail. Jules was dead set on his fist-sized coin said he would make a necklace out of it.

Just before they set off to go, Garth stopped to smoke another cigarette, and this time he walked over to Ernest. Meanwhile, Ernest was giving sheepish glances at the dead woman and absently toeing the dead cat's carcass, watching it rock stiffly with each light kick.

"the meat's no good, Ern. It would make us sick if we tried to eat it."

Ernest knew that, but the sight of it, brought back a curious memory.

As a younger boy, before he'd been chosen for the Convent's militia, his family had a barn, or maybe it was a small shed. Inside it one day, there had been a cat, a long orange one, and she had birthed a litter of kittens. He remembered how they'd mewed and wriggled blindly against her swollen stomach looking for a teat to suckle from. He remembered how his dad had been happy because they would keep mice away. Ernest found that strange because he couldn't remember what his dad's voice sounded like, but he remembered all the rest of that.

Suddenly, a small blur of the motion passed by his periphery, and he turned. Garth was clutching his pack of cigarettes but open and with the little sticks pointed towards Ernest.

"Go ahead." He urged. Slowly Ernest reached out and plucked one, placing it between his lips. And before he knew Garth was holding a zippo up under its tip. Ernest took a sharp breath and exhaled, hacking at the deep earthy burn in his throat and lungs.

Garth let out a little chuckle.

"Come on, Ern, time to get stepping to take point."

Ernest nodded and took an easier pull this time. He hardly coughed when he breathed out. He threw one more look at the bloated feline at his feet. Its stomach was swollen too, but not with milk. He cocked his leg back and gave it a swifter kick sending it rolling and tumbling into the wide, darkening pool of blood and congealed brains stretching from the corpse's head that no longer looked like the woman who was pleading earlier. With a shattered skull giving it structure, the head had collapsed and looked more like an exquisite Halloween mask than a thinking, speaking, scared person. Soon Ernest's feet carried him away, and he wondered how long before she too would be bloated like the roadkill she'd carried.

Just past midday, they'd neared the bridge they were supposed to clear for the troopers that would be coming down the interstate it spanned over.

Just a hazy 800 some meters away, they'd made good time considering the hang-ups this morning. Or at least that's what garth told them. "Let's see if Jokem is still at the bar, huh?" Garth said with some face splitting enthusiasm.

Jokem was a bartender and roadside merchant who had been here in the winter the last time the Foot team had been in this part of the territory. It seemed like Jokem had known one of Garths old Team leaders, and for that, he had always treated them nicely. Last time he gave Garth a whole bottle of some booze without garth even pulling his gun out. The last time he'd tried it, Ernest had just felt sick and dizzy, but maybe this time, he'd have as much fun as other people seemed to when they drank it.

But as they approached the brown shingled building, Garth lost his enthusiasm.

"Little yellow-bellied fuck." He swore when he neared the boardedup bar. "Didn't he think some warfighters would want some booze? He ran out when business would've been best. What a fucking moron."

He tried to peer through the boards and into the window past them. James spoke up.

"Well, if he boarded up, that means he's tryna keep squatters away, so he'll probably be back some time." Garth waved away the notion.

"That don't do us any fuckin good. I want some booze and fresh food now!" he let out a long sigh and gripped one of the boards. "Well, come on, let's get these boards out of our way. There's probably some shit left in here.

They obeyed the four of them working in a few minutes if silence pulling and banging on boards until enough had been torn away to expose a window.

"Doors probably locked anyway," Garth said with a wink as he bent to pick up a piece of busted concrete that had been laying stagnant on the sidewalk outside the building beside timeless cigarette buts and other bits of rubbish. With a smooth movement, he hurled it into the glass with a satisfying crash of breaking glass.

"Alright, watch out for the sharp bits. Get your asses in there.

And a few moments later, they were inside the bar searching for leftover bottles amongst stowed chairs and empty shelves. Just when it seemed like Jokem had absconded with all of his property. Garth emerged from behind the bar with a three-quarters full misty bottle of clear liquid.

"Storytime boys!" he called out, twisting the metal cap free while he procured three cups and took a drag strait from the bottle himself. He was wincing when he drew his lips away and letting out a painful hiss.

"Goddamn, that kicks!" they all saddled up to the bar as he poured them each a little bit of the pungent clear liquid. The swill flooded Ernest's head with an antiseptic smell that made him warry to sip from the cup. Julius had no such reservations and tried to down his all in one go. This led him to a gagging hacking fit that Garth found particularly hilarious. But soon, they all settled back down and looked to Garth for the inevitable story he'd already mentioned. Ernest had heard the story of his scar enough to tell it himself, but he knew better than to cut in on such tradition.

Garth leaned both elbows on the dusty bar and asked.

"Now, where was I last night?"

James, who sat hunched under the weight of his pack; he never let it drop from his shoulders until their patrols were done, spoke up.

"You were talking about the machine gun. It had just tore up a lot of them footboys like us." For the first time, Ernest realized that James must've heard this story even more times than he himself had and wondered how he kept so rapt upon its retelling.

"That's right!" Garth began his smile growing complete and nasty.
"The damned thing was so loud I hardly knew what to do at first. I didn't even realize them; boys were getting shredded the way they were." He took another swig.

"Made that mess we left on the road look clean when you compares em. Anyhow, I had me a good Team leader just like y'all. He pushed us into a side alley so that machine gun wouldn't keep tearing us up but..." and he let the but hang in the air for theatrics just how he always did, sweeping his gaze across the boys in front of him until it fell upon Julius. The latter hadn't been subject to its continuous retelling.

"He didn't know it was all a trap, and BAM!" he slapped his hand down onto the bar top to drive home the survive. Ernest allowed himself a small moment of pride that he hadn't flinched this time.

"From the rooftops up above came a few gunshots and these flaming bottles that busted up all around us lighting boys on fire Lordy was they screaming!" he said solemnly as he took another apparently painful pull from the bottle. When he had gulped and fought to keep it down, he kept going. "But, Dylan... my lead, he was still moving. One side lit on fire as he moved toward Ricky, who was slumped against the wall tryna hold his guts together where a slug had split em."

"Joey, ignoring the fire licking him up and down and Ricky's screaming, he goes and grabs the grenade off the footboys vest, and what's that sonafabitch do?"

Garth didn't wait for any of them to try and answer. He twisted his torso and levied his arm back like he was about to throw a world record shotput through the bar's roof.

"He lobs that thing all the way up to the roof, and BOOM! It goes off. It blows up the rest of their little fire bottles, and the whole building shakes and BURNS!"

He leaned forward again and pulled the mop of messy brown hair back from his forehead to show a little streaking star-shaped scar near his hairline.

"One of the bricks hit me right there. And then a mess of that burning oil fell onto my back, giving me that other scar, but when the smoke cleared, I was the only one left." Expectedly, he let the pause run as if the story was over, but Ernest heard the next line before he spoke it like a well-worn record. *"Well, almost the only one..."*

"Well, almost the only one. When I pulled myself to my feet and patted the fire off me, I saw some moving peoples. Just a few feet ahead was one of them from the roof. He was somehow still alive. Fucker was holding his little shit-eating buddy in his lap who had a hunk of rebar gutting him. Oh, they were muttering some nonsense about being okay and getting outta there, but they ain't see me."

"I couldn't find my rifle though, so I had to be real smart about it.
There between us was Joey's burnt up body and..." he pulled his pistol out of its holster and gestured it around. "His revolver!" Garth called out triumphantly.

"I pulled it free and gunned those two fucks down before they knew what was happening!"

Now, he gestured to the butte of the grip where two blemishes showed. Little tally marks scraped into the glossy checkered wood handle.

"That's where them two came from." He said with a practiced pride. Then a realization sparked, and his grin spread again.

"Guess, I get to add another one!" he said with a cackle.

The boys sat silently, sipping the remainder of their drinks like it was a chore. All while Garth used the bowie knife to delicately scrape a new mark into the butte of the pistol. Ernest figured that was the closest thing to a headstone she'd get. Then Ernest realized he didn't seem to care. He didn't seem to care about anything, and that seemed pretty alright. He didn't even notice that James had slipped off to go use the bathroom. And he didn't notice that James had taken a long time in that bathroom visit.

"Hey! Jul! look for James! We've spent too much time fucking off here." Garth slurred as he slipped the knife and pistol back into their assigned seats at his hips.

"Sure thing," Jules said, slipping off his seat and walking behind Ernest with a little bit of a stagger as he did.

When Jules made it to the other side of the room, Garth drew close to the spot in front of Ernest and looked into his eyes.

"That gives us a second to talk."

Ernest gulped and looked back into Garth's bleary eyes.

"You know what wuddah happened if I'd been a little pussy like you that day in the alley?"

Ernest didn't know whether nodding was the right move, but the question ended up rhetorical, and Garth rambled on.

"They'd ah killed me dead like the rest of em. Then you know what wuddah happen to you?"

This time Ernest shook his head, which was the right answer. Garth leaned over the bare until less than a foot was between their faces before he spoke next.

"That dirty cunt on the road wuddah skinned and eaten you with a side of kitty cat stew. You can't wait, you can't second guess, or they'll split you wide open, then they'll keep killing the rest of us two. Is that what you want?"

Before Ernest could respond with a "no, sir." A shrill scream came from the bar's back hallway where Julius had gone to look for James. Their prior conversation was forgotten quickly at the hair-raising sound. Both of the boys at the bar ran towards the hallway, weapons at the ready. Ernest reached the hallway first and saw Jules shrinking back from the open bathroom door, his back pressed against the opposite wall, and his mouth agape. The young boy looked at Ernest with a pale horror-stricken face that seemed to silently plead to wipe what it had just witnessed from history. The two boys were each locked in a place. One frozen by horror already seen and by the terror of what he might perceive if he continued down the hallway.

Behind him, Garths' pounding footfalls were drowned out by Julius's breathless sobs trying to articulate his pain.

"He's...He's. Not, he." But he couldn't string the words together, and finally, pure nervous energy drove him in a panic from his spot on the wall, and he went tearing down the hall and past the still frozen Ernest. Once again, Ernest found himself willing his body to move. To step down the hallway. But something stopped him. This time it was a clear but a source less sense of futility. Some instinct told him that strolling down the stained and peeling hallway would result in nothing good. It was apparent Garth had no such instinct and threw himself past the stagnant boy and down the hall until disappearing into the small one-person bathroom on the right-hand side.

A roaring chorus of curses erupted out of the room, as well as a few questions.

"Where the Fuck is his Pack... or his gun?!" well, Ernest didn't rightly know the answer to those inquiries. Followed shortly by.

"Ernest! What the fuck are you doing? Get down here!" Ah, now that was a simpler request, and as reluctant as he was a moment ago, he bid his feet to move and this time, they complied. Bringing him to the doorway, allowing him to peer into the bathroom at his second corpse of the day (third counting the damn cat).

Just past Garth's hunched form was the ragdoll formerly known as James. His head was a pulpy ruin of what it once was, and his lips and skin had turned this horrid blue/purple showing he'd choked to death after getting the absolute hell beat out of his little round skull. Not only that, but his neck was canted at a weird angle as if it had been snapped. The whole scene came together to erase the silent, helpful boy Ernest had come to know and replace him with this weird asphyxiated fishboy with swollen lips and discolored parlor.

"Go find Julius! Whoever did this has the fucking pack and James' gun!"

Ernest nodded and plodded back down the hall. The present danger shook him from his stupor, and he found himself tucking his rifle to his shoulder and keeping his head on a sweeping swivel as he looked about the bar for Julius. He nearly called out for him but thought against it as it might draw the killer's attention. Instead, he assumed Jules wanted to get as far away from the scene. Naturally, this would've taken him outside.

Crawling back out the window, sure enough, he found Jules sitting hugging his knees tight with his back to the outer wall and his skinny rifle at his feet. Ernest could hear here his teammate's great heaving sobs that were turning to wails that shook his slender frame.

Ernest stopped right in front of him, searching for the words to say and finding none.

"Jules…" he started, the sound of his voice seemed so deadpan and alien. But it was enough to at least lift Julius's head from up to look at Ernest. Tears had been pouring freely from the boy's deep brown eyes, smearing the grime they all carried and sending little rivulets down the boy's smooth and freckle spotted features.

Then a deafening *CRACK* split the air, and Julius's head twisted at an alarming speed to his left. A familiar blur of red was caught in Ernest's periphery as he spun rifle in hand towards the report.

There! At the edge of the building was a large sulking figure that had leaned out from the corner of the bar's exterior. Reflexively, Ernest squeezed hard on the trigger letting a quaking burst of fire rattle from his weapon at the receding form. The bullets only hit empty air and the stucco siding of the building. As silence flooded back into the space created by the gunfire, Ernest inched towards the corner he'd seen the attacker disappear behind.

"Fucking shit! Ernest, stop!" he heard from behind him. Against every instinct in his body, Ernest peeled his vision away from the corner to look over his shoulder. Only to see Garth clambering out of the window. The team leader quickly gained his footing and shuffled to Julius's sprawled form.

For the first time since the recent attack, Ernest looked at his downed comrade as well. The bullet had smashed into the boy's jaw, completely obliterating the lower half of Julius' face leaving only a flayed red ruin with shattered bits of teeth and bone protruding from the pulp in shades of pink and white. The worst part was that he wasn't dead. No Jules was continuing his attempts at

67

breathing, at crying, at living in the most grotesque way. With no bottom jaw, his tongue lulled about worm-like below a bubbling hole that was his blood choked throat.

"Ern, go inside, get your pack," Garth said softly. His own hand was now shaking while it drifted down to the handle of his bowie knife.

"But…" Ernest began.

"NOW!" Garth roared as the knife slid free and began to raise over Julius's heaving chest.

Ernest clutched his rifle tight for security and turned to go in but not before hearing a sickening, wet *Crunch* of a blade punching through a young boy's sternum. He flowed his last order autonomously. It seemed like the only way to go about things in a time like this. Hurriedly, he tightened his pack down onto his back and looked up towards the window to see Garth mid pistol draw. What came next was a series of sounds ranging from subtle to cacophonous.

A creak of a floorboard behind him, the ragged breath of a grown man bearing down on him, the gut-wrenching thump of something metal smashing against his head and reverberating through his skull. Then there was the sound of a gunfight that sounded far away and drowned out by some kind of running water or rushing wind. Thankfully, blissful silence pervaded as his consciousness fled him.

He awoke, wishing to slip back to the black when a crushing headache immediately met him. It took him a few moments to piece together what must have happened. The hidden assailant, obviously a vicious enemy trooper, had picked off his Foot Team and waylaid him. He had to go...

somewhere.

He had to do something. But what? What would Garth do?

Well, after anything remotely interesting, he'd radio up to "Higher," but Ernest didn't have a radio. He had to find Garth, see if he was still alive.

He finally pushed past the headache and roused himself to a sitting position. Sure enough, the unseen man had taken his rifle, but he had left him his pack. He pivoted, feeling something dip into his stomach. Yes! Tucked into his belt was the revolver from earlier. Ernest flipped open the cylinder with bated breath, and sure enough, two unfired bullets sat snugly ready to be loosed.

He tightened his hold on the cracked grip and fought dizziness as he pushed himself to his feet. For a moment, he wanted to run, to hide, maybe to just collapse again into a ball on the floor. But no, the pistol felt good in his hand—no shaking this time, no hesitating.

Slowly, at first, until his feet returned to him, he walked towards that window. No to obvious a course. He doubled back. There must have been some other way the enemy trooper was getting in and out of here. Between splitting aches, he was able to piece together an idea: James, the bathroom.

He stumbled his way down the hall and into the bathroom. Ignoring his teammate's twisted corpse, he looked up, and sure enough, a small window was propped open, letting the mid-afternoon sun filter into the horrid room. With no little effort, Ernest vaulted himself up and caught the lip. With an excruciating attempt, he pulled himself up and through the window, falling unceremoniously out into the bar's backlot. He scrambled to his feet and spun, looking around for any sign of danger but found none. He peered around the corner at the surrounding buildings. A long burned out gas station was closest to him but seemed to offer no real safety or purpose to his attacker. Beyond that, a roadside motel, maybe? But this man had to have a sense something brought him here just as they had.

The bridge. They'd been sent to secure this bridge so that the Convents troopers wouldn't be bothered on their march south. If this man were a trooper from an enemy militia, he would be doing the opposite. Ernest didn't give himself any time to be proud of his revelations as he began running towards the bridge. He knew what must be done now.

As he neared the unceremonious concrete bridge, he found himself creeping low with eyes wide, hunting for a sign of his quarry. And he saw them just as he stepped onto the bridge, maybe 10-15 meters away from him with his back turned.

The man squatted; his broad back was draped with a dark cloak whose ends hung in muddy tatters. The trooper's hair was grimy and black, not unlike Ernest's when he grew it out. Along the bridge's edges were laid his team's weapons to aide in a single man ambush on a larger force. The man could slink between weapons while in cover to fire from a new location without reloading. Just over his shoulder, he could see Garth. Still alive but bound and beaten. At the moment, the man held a small revolver in his right hand and the blocky radio in the left. Both of them aimed at Garth, who looked close to tears.

All Ernest had to do was get a little closer. He only had two bullets, and he wanted to make sure he didn't miss it. He advanced, pistol raised with his gaze flipping between the man's back and Garth's face. That was his mistake. Garth ignored whatever the trooper was trying to get him to do with the radio and looked dead at Ernest. This alerted his enemy's keen senses causing the man to spin and face the skulking boy. Everything began to flow in slow motion flashes.

The man turned and looked at Ernest, his eyes growing in surprise at that moment. Something eerily familiar struck him about the man, but it didn't have time to float up to the forefront of his mind.

Next, seeing a window of opportunity, Garth, resourceful to the end, rocked forward head butting the man with all his force and sending him staggering back, nearly falling.

Ernest held his fire, not wanting to hit his team leader in the momentary scuffle, but as the two pulled apart, he nearly squeezed until he saw the man's face, and the creeping familiarity came back, giving him pause.

"FUCKING KILL HIM!" Garth squealed. Any attempts at bravado or command were forgotten in his distress as he was still bound hand and foot. The sound was closer to a cry to God; than it was to any earthly being.

But the other man spoke with a chillingly, calm voice.

"Ernest." The way he said his name brought shivers to Ernest's spine. It felt wrong. He didn't know why, but it felt just deeply wrong as if he was never meant to hear it spoken by this tongue.

"Ernest," he continued, "I'm sorry you weren't supposed to be out here. I thought you'd be out for longer. Just walk away, Ernest."

The name, his name. Why did it cut him so deeply? Was it with how this man spoke?

"Fucking kill this psycho Ern; he's goddamn crazy he is! WHAT ARE YOU WAITING FOR!" Garth kept squealing and squirming in his bonds.

"I don't Have time to explain this, Ernest. But I'm giving you a chance not just to walk away but to be more than this." He said, beating his own chest then adding, "Then HIM!" The man said, pointing towards the undulating form of Garth on the ground.

"You stupid little pussy kill him! Kill him, or I'll stomp your fucking head into paste! KILL HIM!"

The man took a step towards Ernest, letting his own small chrome revolver clatter to the blacktop.

"I'm so sorry for him, Ernest. I'm sorry for myself. For how things had to be. But you can change all of that." With sickening lucidity, everything shifted into focus—the unplaceable familiarity of the man's face—the words he was saying what he was trying to convey. The duplicity of the beat-up chromeplated pistol he'd dropped. But most of all the way he'd said his name. It was the same tone and cadence with which Ernest introduced himself to others. Like a jolt of electricity, a decision shot from the center of his mind to the tip of his trigger finger.

Not one but two shots rang out on that bridge that afternoon, but only one man died.

LOVE GLORY LUST
HEARTACHE SHAME SIN
(and other addictions)
"This is the part that the thugs skip…"- J.Cole

<u>Chemik</u>

Metabolize and kill me.

Burn and distill me.

Most of all, preserve me.

Embalm my soul if I can't grow; then I'm a corpse.

Just keep the decay away. I wanna die whole.

Aneurysm Overlooked

I feel that you're obsessed with my obsession.

You love my passion but not the heart that beats behind it.

Drunk to the rhythm of the beat but blind to the
blood that leaks.

<u>Metallurgy</u>

Iron sharpens iron, this I've always known,

But what happens when you're a diamond and I'm as soft as gold.

My Dream

My body curled itself into one of those contorted mockeries of a sleeper's pose that anyone with a familiarity with the infantry or another vagabond lifestyle might know and have found themselves in at some point. The kind that run's the razor's edge between comfort and complete permanent deformity of the spine. The end result is always being a feverish sleeplike state of mind serves more like a mechanic to catapult one's self further in time than to provide actual rest.

It was this that drove my mind to make the bastard child of a half-baked daydream and the desperate longing of someone who doesn't know if he is heartbroken.

Whatever else, the dream was sunny. Seemingly lit by warm natural light flowing in from windows that never came into focus or detail and that's fine with me given the tradeoff. All else I can say of my surreal surroundings were benefitting from windows and seemed to be traveling of its own accord as if I was on a train, plane, or maybe even a bus. I was seated on a bench or some sort of couch and most importantly, truly as it blotted out any other detail, she was with me.

She was lounging with her head resting in my lap. The fully realized image of a beautiful idea and nothing more. As at the time our distance, physical and personal, had barred us from the opportunity to create memories for this dream to draw from. Nevertheless, I was quite familiar with her face and the dream spared no expense in reminding me.

The features of it stood like a landscape that engulfs your soul leaving you feeling small in the face of nature's glory. Its own details bearing pieces of both strength and delicacy that rather than crash in any disjointed homeliness, instead danced hand in and cheek to cheek to create one of the most striking of visages that deny any others a chance at female beauty. Her eyes were the same ice blue that warns my heart of so much danger yet demand the attention and silent devotion of the rest of me.

Full and shimmering hair of dark auburn that flaunts a regal promise of pedigree only seen in polished mahogany. It fell listless and flowing about my lap with any attempt to keep it orderly completely ignored and the look on her face told me why.

It was a look I'd never seen on her face and my dreams attempt at it bordered on uncanny.

She was smiling.

Not just smiling, but beaming with euphoric wonder. The kind of smile that serves to separate bouts of pure joyous laughter. The kind of smile that punctuates a well-received and reciprocated confession of undying love.

And she was smiling at me, with one of my hands framing her face and her hand holding it there like it was the keystone holding her together.

There was nothing else to the dream. No idea or inference as to the topic of our conversation. No knowledge. No knowledge of that, no all of that was eradicated from memory to make room for the beauty of that moment. Waking, I feared it might slip from my mind as dreams do. So, I grabbed my pen in the hopes of immortalizing it, and now as the task draws to a close, a new one hangs over me. My duty to fulfill this prophecy.

<u>Calloused</u>

Maybe it was how starkly her skin stood out against mine.

Was she an anomaly? Could she really be something so tender and alien that my mind began tearing itself apart to understand her?

Or I have I just grown that calloused?

Focus

I want this to change before the death of me.

What was once the end goal of a cavalcade of half-baked nights, I wish to be the transition between the rest of my days.

A savage topic once the chest-beating bravado of animals.

I want to be a solitary conspiracy so deeply draped in secrecy that crowds shudder to think what it might be.

Or to knock it from its lauded pedestal to disseminate and translate until the masses know it inside and out.

I wish this to be a meditation, not idolatry.

Long Face

How many times do you end up here?

A muddy reflection in a glossy bar top with music too loud to hear a single thought.

But you don't wanna hear those anyway. You already know the story by god you wrote it.

So, you sit here sporting a frown and more drinks then the couples to your left and right.

You know if you look sad enough, the bartender might give you pity at the end of the night.

Hindsight

I want to see your world so that I'll never question.

Your love for a scared boy learning to be more than man.

<u>LUST</u>

It's made a liar of me.

The way it pushes and cajoles until love lays cold.
A murderer with a jester's face turns me to an
accomplice with more empty promises.

I watch in fool's motley as it smothers all honesty.

I follow along as it's conspirator until it's painted my
face and twisted my smile.

Now, I find myself at the end of a roadmap of sin and
I fit the killer's profile.

Moments

You're every time I looked at a lonely bottle and didn't give it comfort.

You're the times I dream that they'll build statues to me.

You've given my ego a playground with a target on its back with that I found space from my greatest enemy.

Every instance of strength can be carbon dated to the moment you turned your eyes towards me.

But you know as well as me, these moments are not eternity and that bottle won't stay lonely, but I know you'll kill it with me.

<u>Two praying hands</u> frame
my head as my lap becomes
                        your alter.
        Those fingers run through my curls like they're
        searching for scriptures.

        This new religion offers no salvation

        That's okay, we know eternity in the small moments.

Necrophile I spin up the ghost of love's long dead though in truth they were stillborn.

I find solace in what would have been and gloss their failures in rose tints until a fully formed specter is conjured. Enough-

Soon I'm flayed by a twin forked tongue of lies I've told and lies I was sold.

Her rose tint only reflects it never refracts to shine any new light on past acts.

spirits

What's inside you is
inside of me.
Bottled and packaged for distribution.

And when that cork is twisted or that tab is lifted the
poison flows until the bottle is empty

But the damage stays. Scars on a liver, scars on a
mind, and scars on any heart attached to mine.

Instincts shifting

-I woke up confused in a dark room-

-no light could be found-

-the old instincts came late- -

where?

-how?

-they didn't cross my mind-

-only the why-

-Why were you not by my side?

Her Weapon

Rough around the edges, but she holds me like a weapon.

White knuckle grip like I'm her only protection.

Whether it's from herself or this world, it isn't clear to me.

But God help em if she ever unsheathes me.

Ragana

You're it

You're a heart eating bitch

I watch it drip

From your tongue

From your lips

Down your chin, now spit

Now spray

Disseminate me to mist

You're it

You're a witch

I feel my atoms split under your kiss

Logic dies in this superstitious light

All belief and reason passes

Replaced with spellbound devotion

You're it

You're the end of me

A death I've begged for between these sheets

A devil summoned and shackled but also ripped free

You're it

The target of my sin

It's not a fairy tale ending for this love is grim

But it's not us who should shiver since this horror shall not end

Trinity

I am He

Searching my own fault lines for the cracks that drove
her to the beds of better men.

I am He

Who turns hurt and self-harm loose with a
whoreson's soul on every barstool hopeful knowing
I've got love at home?

I am He

A soul laying apathetic as ego takes the reigns
running rampant past banded hands and bedstand
portraits swell it with pride as if she wouldn't just
pin another to her bedside. I am He

I am trinity

Bearing this degradation for eternity

THING

    -My eyes race and roll with frantic looks as a
realization looms over a barren room-

-not a thing means a thing, I'm devoid of all ties to these
things
I've been gifted, stolen, or gone to buy-

        -tools of my trade sit lifeless in wait

     -clothes that I've got seem crumpled and fake

       -uniforms most days just suffocate

-Not a ribbon, nor a pin, no symbol of rank-

  -All of it ash, trash, and rubbish mounting high above as if
                              to topple me-

    -I dig low looking for something, something,
something must mean something. From my pocket comes
a wallet well worn. Looking inside I find no bills, no
money, no coin. Only a lone ticket stub and the pain of a
boy-

     -from a movie theater, from a date long

    before- -a memory of hope ahead of

    being a whore-

      -of the first girl to be giving-

-who caught glimpse of my hate and answered it grinning-

      -but I know how it ended-

       -the things that I did-

-so, before I give it to

the fire- -i

scrawled on it-

Fin.

Toxicity

I looked at you like medicine, breathing hopes into my life again.

Inflating beliefs that had long fell slack from disuse.

Then the promises fell from sky to refuse and now truth shines through on your serums side effects.

I'm left torn by your needlework.

Curdled blood now barley slogs through a sluggish heart to dash hopes against veins turned varicose.

This was an addiction, not salvation.

All I wish is to know myself again, not this nervous junky scared to leave the hell you put him in.

Strait Edge

It cuts like a razor, that's why these guys like me
knock our heads back and cackle at sobriety.

It rises shrill as a banshee's scream only to be
drowned out by a chemical static that obscures any
truth about our bad habits.

But it's the headaches and foggy days that drain any
hope found in the dates not yet reached.

The cold turkey treatment might turn my condition
terminal.

That ain't nothing new, spending my all my nights
sharing a bed with the reaper and see his grim
demeanor in every mirror

Even if it throws my psyche in the crypt. I'll just rise
on the other side into the moonlight

Y   A minuscule cosmic incident occurred on my knuckles by accident.

That lonely finger on the left hand had been left
unbothered for some time.

Now it can't hide it's since been emblazoned with
such a startling Y.

Y is it so bare of any martial metallurgy?

Y do I imagine weddings with hopeful wives only
to leave them before the alters can be built?

Y do I care at an age like

this? Y do I care in an age

like this?

Y is such a small thing growing so big?

Defeat

Cigarettes in the rain,

I didn't win this time, but I'll start again Monday.

Smoke explores my hollows while cold pinpricks
outline my mortal frame.

I wonder if this is what it takes to be complete, but
my mind is full of its own heresy.

Grey skies loom wrestling for eternity while I ponder
if art is only born of pain.

I stand statuesque while my head rumbles with

hungover fits. I'll make coffee and go about my

day. After I stop smoking this cigarette in the rain.

DEATH IN THE AFTERNOON

The Cantina could be a comfortable place if you let it, Carter.

Yes, he supposed it very well could be; but its slopping brick walls and stucco ceiling reminded him of a pizza oven he'd seen as a pimple-faced teen working the food industry. The ridiculous imagery of an oven door slamming shut, and a dial turning up the temperature made him tug at the collar of his shirt.

The oven idea wasn't the only one making him want to run out of here and disappear into the desert dunes. Maybe some leather-skinned nomad tribes might toss some pity his way and welcome him in. He could be their dumb little pet and would amuse them with his alien ways.

He was still barely a ferry ride away from the European conflict he was fleeing, and he was undoubtedly sure plenty of its players had extended the game south as they always had for centuries. That begged the question of where he was to run to?

His eyes canvased the room in the same nervous pattern he'd been
perfecting over the past month. It was one of those little tricks you learned when you'd survived being on the losing side. That was why he was so startled that he felt a small tap on his shoulder during this self-induced paranoia.

"Your taste is rather out of fashion, don't you think?" the voice
was
unspeakably foreign in its accent and enticing in its cadence.

He turned quickly, visions of a snub nose already pointing at his temple dancing through his mind expecting that his mind would be dancing through the air any second. No, it was something far worse than a gun.

Indeed, a woman drawn from universal ideas of eroticism and beauty that permeated all cultures stood before him—wrapped up in a tight crimson dress, making her curves a spectacle, not a mystery.

Carter's gaze flowed up past the curves and bust to a regal face made unreadable except in its bemusement. Perhaps this was because the combination of brown liquor and her beauty was obscuring his intuition. She was definitely a local. The sharp facial features and prominent nose spoke of a lineage that had seen countless pasty conquerors and explorers come and go. If he was in a more philosophical mind state, he might wonder where he fell between those paradigms.

She let out an impatient sigh.

"Well?" she asked, throwing a gaze at the empty chair across from him.

"How'd you know not to use English? What if

I was Dutch? " She let out a small chuckle and

rolled her eyes.

"Only Americans travel halfway around the world to drink cheap whiskey neat by themselves."

He tipped the glass towards the chair in the invitation, which she accepted with liquid grace. When she was lounging in the dark leather highback, he prodded her lie.

"And how'd you know this whiskey is cheap?" he said, swirling it over the flickering fake candle between them for more precise inspection.

"If you must know, asked the bartender." She said, the smile earlier bemused began to spread further, casting excited folds across her smooth cheeks that formed into dimples.

"And why would he share that with you?" he said, taking a sip of the admittedly cheap whiskey. Granted, cheap whiskey did the same job as the expensive ones.

"If your boss asks you a question, don't

you answer?" He chuckled for a

moment.

"You're the owner of this place? For how long."

"Since I was eight technically speaking."

"How'd you come into such good fortune?" he asked, trying not to let his curiosity become genuine. Just because the invitation of sex was seemingly dangled in front of him on a string, he should still be keeping a level head. Her smile turned contemptuous.

"A dead mother, and by association a dead grandmother. Are you about finished with that swill?"

He knocked the rest back and laid the empty glass between them.

"Is barkeeping a business all the dead matrons of your family undertake?"

As she spoke, she waved over one of the tuxedoed waiters that seemed so tacky to Carter when he'd first sat down.

"Not really. This was a healer's house for five centuries, believe it or not, I had to make some adaptations, of course."

As the silly little man neared, carter dug deeper.

"Hmm, quite the change of direction you took."

When he neared, she spoke to him in French words that he couldn't quite decipher. All he could derive was that it was expressed with politeness he rarely heard from French speakers. The two smiled at each other, and the waiter nodded before disappearing.

"Not hardly." She said, returning to their conversation with a furrowed brow, "Is this not a place of healing, Monsieur…?"

"Burke. And I suppose if you see slow euthanasia as healing, then yes, quite the healing hut you have here."

She let out what seemed to be a genuine laugh of amusement.

"Quite the cynic, M.Burke. Is that why you aren't wearing your ring?" Oh, the venom in that question! It might have wounded him personally a few months ago, but right now, it was hard to ignore the danger posed by someone with such personal knowledge of him without him having any experience of them. Even though a slimy sensation of fear crept his spine, he kept his face and inflections stoic.

"Did your bartender tell you that too, missus…?"

"Bohm, Miss Bohm," she said, leaning forward to cup her chin in her left hand and wiggle the fingers of it tauntingly, showing how free they were of such fetters. Marital status was the least of carter's concern. Her last name told a much more sinister story. He tilted his head in curiosity before speaking again

"You wouldn't be related to...?" she cut him off with heavy boredom at the forefront of her tone.

"Hector Bohm? Yes, he is my father, and to answer your other question. No, my workers didn't tell me that you did." She waited a moment for him to register his confusion. That name carried weight. Eurolog was the logistics wing of the Centralist state ran enterprises in Europe. Hector was one of its chairmen and the overseer of its Extra-atmospheric shipping. Carter had seen firsthand what those suborbital vehicles could "Ship" when the company had turned plowshares to swords. This was an interesting turn.

"Well, your little tan line did." She said, reaching over to tap the place on his ring finger where his wedding band had rested for the entirety of the Iberian conflict and even up to a few days prior. Sure enough, the sun lashed skin he'd garnered over the past few years was split by a paler band of flesh that her middle and index finger now stroked ever so lightly, making the hairs from his arm to his neck stand on end.

"Aren't you perceptive?" He stated flatly, closing his hand into a fist and drawing it to his lap.

She scoffed and rolled her eyes.

"Don't get sanctimonious now. Your eyes haven't been faithful to you or Mrs. Burke; where Is she, by the way?"

"I wouldn't know." He said flatly

She leaned back in the chair, crossed her arms.

"Oh well, too bad for her, and stop being so gruff. If you've got the audacity to play at infidelity, then you might as well be brazen about it."

"I never said anything of the sort."

She huffed impatiently and craned her slender neck to peer past him. All while muttering.

"you didn't have to."

She eyed the waiter returning to their table with two tall, fluted glasses of bubbling, and ever so slightly green, fluid with a floating star of anise in each one. She thanked the waiter in French once more and took both of the glasses into her hands.

"Which one do you want, M. Burke? You're a nervous man, and I don't want you fretting over poisons or drugs," she said matter of factly.

He looked back and forth between the two glasses before reaching for the left one resignedly.

"thank you, although I can't say I'm a fan of how keen your intuition is." She raised the glass to toast, and with a pleasant smile, she chimed

"Liars never do."

It was his turn to roll his eyes. But he did clink glasses

"I don't think I've lied yet, have I?" he asked.

She held up a finger in response as she hungrily guzzled over a quarter of the drink. Her lips parted from the glass with a pleasant gasp, and once again, carter felt hot under the collar.

"I'm sure you have, but even my intuition has its limits." And then changing the subject, "Are you familiar with the drink? It's an American one."

He could already smell the sickly-sweet licorice floating up on dry notes of champagne.

"Death in the afternoon, but you've gone a bit heavy with absinthe."

She swirled her glass and letting a giggle bubble up, then crooned softly.

"We aren't drinking for health, Mr. Burke."

"So much for a healing house." With that, he knocked back a mouthful of what turned out to be a rather delightful drink.

"And it's Carter, by the way." He added after swallowing.

"Well, Carter Burke. Go ahead and tell me what's brought you here."

"Leaving here is what's brought me here. I'm not

staying long." "What a shame." She said with a

pout and another sip.

"You'll have to find some other little plaything. I'm sure that's not hard for you."

This brought the smile back and made her lower the drink to the table.

"Don't debase me so, I could up and leave, you know." She said with a downward glance.

As she did, she ran her pointer finger over the rim of the fluted glass. The sight brought the image of a feline playing with a mouse it had yet to kill. This woman was dangerous. That was an unavoidable fact. But what did the daughter of a Eurolog chairman want with him? He'd been little more than a mercenary in the Iberian conflict, hardly worth attention for the most part. However, he was labeled as a terrorist by the centralists. Maybe she worked in a different wing than her father? One that was willing to do some wet work and was here to serve some new world justice.

"Then leave." He stated as if it was the simplest solution to whatever had caused their paths to collide. And god, how he wanted her to get up and walk away. He supposed that bastard knew how much he didn't as well.

"You're handsome, Carter, in a cookie-cutter way, at least. This little cynic act of yours probably works wonders on some people, I'm sure. But, you won't find a better company than me if I leave this table."

He shrugged.

"Maybe I enjoy my own company?" he proposed.

"A liar indeed," she purred in her amalgam of an accent that carried the breathy flow of something akin to French. Maybe she'd studied there? But each word ended with a cut of the local tongue and perhaps a sprinkle of her father's Germanic one.

"How so?" this was dragging on. It was so painfully apparent he should leave. But what then? Be

127

waylaid in the street by rough handed thugs? Even if he made it away, there was only a life of running ahead. Maybe this was the best ending his freedom could hope for. Here with a beautiful woman and a drink in hand. What a romanticized way to go out. It was only fitting as he'd romanticized himself into this mess, Into that war, Out of his marriage.

"Cynics don't enjoy their own company. They are cursed by it." With that, her face became alarmingly somber and downcast, "Which is always sad. Cynicism only shows up when sentimentalism has started to die."

Carter wasn't sure what to do with that other than take another healthy swig. Finally, he settled on something.

"What's your name Miss Bohm," he asked, not even realizing his tone had softened until the words escaped him.

"Kahina," she said

"That's a very pretty name."

She was silent for a moment before meeting his gaze.

"Much prettier than Carter," she mused. He felt her high heel play up the leg of his slacks.

"I agree wholeheartedly." He said, reaching down and catching her ankle in his grip. He gave it a small squeeze, then let it free to run back to the floor.

"And there is nothing that might keep you in our little city?" she said, the playful pout returning.

"Well, I could maybe be persuaded. What did you have in mind, Kahina?"

Her face brightened, and the corners of her glossy lips turned up.

"You must see the city from the rooftop bar. The sun will be setting over the water soon, and it is a wonderful sight."

Carter, who wasn't aware that this bar had a rooftop portion, decided it sounded like an excellent place to get black bagged as any.

"Sure, that sounds like it might keep me." She raised her glass at that, and he returned the gesture, and the two met with a soft *tink*

They finished their glasses swiftly and rose from the table. Standing on equal footing, the difference in size between them was stark. At first glance, Carter's height and broad frame seemed capable of engulfing Kahina's sleeker form despite all her dynamism and smothering charisma. Yet when she offered her arm, Carter hooked his through and was lead diligently across the room.

She pulled him along through a sea of tables, all populated by a mix of foreigners and locals who, for just a moment, seemed to turn a blind eye to the encroaching wars and refugee tidal waves to instead make revelry their business. After reaching the other side, she led him to a corner that harbored an easy to miss nook with a small wrought iron staircase that spiraled up into the ceiling.

Kahina slipped her arm from his and began up the stairs stopping after a moment to make sure he was coming. He, of course, was right on her heels. The staircase led into a small, darkly lit room with an open doorway shielded only by a gentling rustling tapestry. Carter was only able to see its details for a moment before they passed, though. An off-white base with a pattern of exquisite colors extending from its center. Yellow, red, and a dull bronze lanced from the center with distinct linear patterns before the beams split, beginning to twist and intertwine before falling to a hazy collage and fading into the off-white background.

He was now on a completely open rooftop, being greeted by a darkening azure sky and a distant sun receding behind the bay. Between all these heavenly bodies, an ivory town was sprawling out, still ancient despite the times. To his right was a small crescent-shaped bar big enough only to house one dusky middle-aged bartender and the high-end spirits behind him. He nodded at the pair upon their entry.

To his left was Kahina leaning against a railing facing the bay. The gloss of her dress caught the fleeting daylight setting it afire and did the same to his gaze.

"Come here. I have something I want to show you." She said, beckoning him to her side.

After he'd complied, she raised a hand and pointed out towards the east.

"Do you see it? There isn't a place I go that my father's endeavors don't reach." He followed her hand, and almost a quarter-mile away on the edge of town was a cluster of buildings in stark contrast to the rest of the city. It was a complex with an open campus populated by small warehouses and hangers with a teardrop-shaped structure of curved blue-green glass rising above the rest at its center—a Eurolog EASP (Extra-atmospheric shipping Port). From there, rockets would carry vehicles up to just out of the earth's atmosphere. They'd then re-enter with new trajectories and speed that cut hours down to minutes for the movement of people and supplies. This and the recent and secretive use of EA/Vehicles to use directed energy platforms in concise military strikes. Carter remembered the unholy aftermath he'd seen in Spain of such tactics. Bodies were popping like water balloons in melting vehicles. Buildings were mysteriously turning to cinder and being blamed on gas leaks or bad wiring.

"Not on good terms, I take it?" he inquired.

"As well as a bastard child can be." And in a hushed tone, she added, "And as well as a decentralist can be."

A knowing smile crept upon his face.

"So now, the truth comes out." He said with a harsh laugh.

She huffed overdramatically.

"What does that mean." Typically, such a phrase is one of haughty selfdefense. But the good humor in her voice told him that she was ready and willing to be caught in her little lies.

"You knew my name before I walked into your little bar, didn't you?"

"Yes, and what good fortune for us both that you walked in. It made things so easy."

"well, what is it you want? War hasn't shown up here yet." He grumbled, walking away from her over to the bartender.

"Whatever pilsener you've got, bottled." He demanded. The bartender simply blinked.

"He's not an English speaker." Called Kahina as she strolled over.

"This area is for…special meetings." She added, saddling up to a barstool beside him. "Not for the public."

"Swingers meetings, or the kind of meetings that end with a Centrist drone strike?"

A sad smile spread on her face, and her hand settled on his white cuffed forearm.

"Well, I'm hardly that promiscuous." Then she turned to the bartender and muttered something in a fluid language he'd never heard before. The dark man reached under the bar and pulled out a dark brown beer bottle and a small silver cigarette case.

He cracked the cap off the bottle and placed it on a napkin before sliding it across the bar to Carter. The cigarette case was slid to Kahina. Carter took a healthy draw before meeting Kahina's eyes again.

"Well, it's a malt, but supply lines and money can only go so far." He commented as he sat the beer back down on the napkin.

"You'll want to cut back on that a little bit."

"And why is that? You want your mercenary clear-headed?" he asked snidely.

"No, I want YOU to be clear-headed." She said. Her other hand dropped to his knee. He was beginning to grow tired of whatever game this was.

"Just be frank with what the fuck you want." He said in a low tone.

"6 years ago, you graduated from VMA second of your class academically, in security sciences, with offers to join the American Olympic wrestling team, or take an army commission. You did neither." She said flatly.

"You joined a security firm that took you to South America,

Venezuela, Brazil, Lima, Peru. But you didn't like that work, did you?"

She stared deeply; her eyes were a burning amber that wouldn't let him look anywhere else. Inside, his inner eye was flicking through green horror scenes of villages, favelas, and downtown streets, where protests turned bloody, dissenters' homes were raided on stiflingly hot nights: the bombed-out woodland and mountain homes.

"What was it? The tribes?" she asked, bringing him back to the Moroccan rooftop. He wouldn't answer, so she continued.

"You became a whistleblower, then a criminal, a terrorist a freedom fighter. One man brought the centrist movement in South America back decades, and oh the ripples that had. Asian insurrections popped back up; Europe saw the encroaching influence."

"Didn't mean anything in the end." He said and looked away. He almost had the beer back to his lips when her hand closed on his wrist.

"Stop." The command came from her with a simple strength.

"I don't work for you yet, stop all the pandering and name your price." He said gruffly.

"What happened to all that money I sent up to Spain?" she asked, and when he could only offer a confused look of shock, she smiled until the realization crept in on him.

"You were the financer?" he asked, remembering how mysterious the Iberian campaign had been. No one in the decentralized resistance could figure out where the funds had come from.

"well, technically it was the Eurolog shadow accounts I'd been stealing from, but yes, I was. so you could say you do work for me." He scoffed past the revelation.

"Well, I'll pay my bar tab and be on my way. Find yourself a new killer." He said, pulling free from her grip and guzzling more of the Baltic malt liquor. She looked to the bartender and curtly said something in the mysterious language. Wordlessly the bartender gave a short bow and dismissed himself. Leaving the pair alone on the roof.

"I am not looking for a mercenary." She said each word deliberately.

"I'm looking for sentimentality."

He scoffed, "I'm a cynic, remember? My sentimentality is dead."

"only if you let it." The pleading that appeared in her voice was alarming and countered the character she'd shown him. He took one of her hands in his, reassuringly squeezing it, and sighed.

"Kahina, I don't know if I'm the guy for this anymore." She shook her head.

"Maybe not. We'll have to see."

She slipped her hand from his grasp and grabbed the small silver cigarette case.

"Come with me." She said, standing up from her seat, "let's go to the couches, and I'll show you something. If you still wish to go, I'll make sure you're on the first bus south tomorrow."

Carter sighed, begrudgingly agreeing, and followed her as she led the way to the small circle of simple couches taking up the roof's remaining floor space.

He left the beer and settled in onto the couch close beside her. The dark sheen of her hair obscured her face as she leaned over the case opening it carefully.

"Well, we've been over your story. Let me give you an idea of mine."

"It's obvious you got your father's penchant for research. I was expecting you to rattle off my blood type and school mascot."

She smiled at that and leaned up to reveal a small glass pipe of a rose gold hue with a small bowl at the end cradled in her fingers.

"Yes, that and his curiosity for genetics." She said, laying the pip on the table in front of them and pulling out a small plastic baggy of light brown dust that she poured a small amount of it onto the glass table and began scraping into a pile.

"Is that...." He began to ask only to be cut off by her.

"No. Now focus. Genetics." She said sternly.

"Specifically, I grew fond of it in a botanical sense. Not his strange obsession of human breeding Hector gifted to all his bastard children." She'd produced a small spoon and was filling the bowl up from the pile.
"Graduated with a double major in plant biology and Biochemistry from Universite PSL at 16. Spent the next year here with some of my.... aunts." she raised the packed pipe in one hand and produced a jet lighter in the

other. The lighter flicked a blue gout of flame and inhaled deeply. After a ragged exhale, she continued.

"Then I finished my masters by 21. Not only that, but I'd finished the research on my magnum opus. The Tetowan Flower." She said before taking a deep breath and passing the small pipe to Carter.

"I'm not sure." He said pensively, looking closer at the powder. Now, he could tell it was finely ground fibers that were still smoldering in the pipe.

"Come on; it's very important. Trust me, Carter." She was leaning in close to him, and even over the rising tendril of the smoking pipe, she smelled intoxicating. Temptation whispered cheeky thoughts in his ear. How long had it been? Since he'd been with Valentina, in the bungalow on the beaches at Yucatan. So that put him on about four years' worth a dry spell. He only stopped wearing the ring this past winter, After the emails stopped being returned.

Fuck it all.

He put the pipe to his lips and drew in a sharp, acrid breath that bit his lungs and hinted at the fine flavor of burning plastic. He went into a fit of coughing that brought a small fit of giggles from Kahina, who began patting him on the back as if to help drive the coughs from him. Soon the coughs turned to laughs of his own, and the pats on his back turned to her softly caressing up and down his spine. "We are smoking it's seed pods now." She added between laughs. Then once those subsided, he asked.

"Your magnum opus was…getting high?"

She shook her head, tossing loose curls about her face. She then began emptying and repacking the bowl.

"What a childish way to look at it." She chided.

This flower is a distant cousin to the Datura, both being alkaloid producing perennials, but it was not nearly as strong in its effects. Not until I started working on it. First, genetically creating more potent strands, then discovering the impact of soil and water alkalinity on the alkaloids it produced. But I can prattle on about NMT derivatives and MAOIs all that wouldn't do anything, so I'll just show you."

She put her lips to the pipe once more and inhaled. Only this time, instead of exhaling, she reached out and gripped firmly on Carter's chin pulling him closer. When he was near, she pressed a kiss upon him, her lips full, warm, and hungry. Then came her breath. The same acrid smoke was there but in a weakened state. He inhaled.

He was taking it in, taking her in. His hand shot to her face, grazing it before cupping the back of the head with silken hair spilling between his fingers. The other grasped her hip, pulling her even closer. The tension that had been there all afternoon was obliterated in a single moment.

But It was when they pulled away from that his world began to strip itself away.

He wasn't sitting on a couch anymore. Instead, he found himself straddling a roaring motorcycle cutting down an impossibly bright desert road. As their lips parted, he saw a beautiful, red-lipped blonde with her hair tied back by a matching bandana leaning up from a sidecar. She was smiling in such a strange way it seemed to extend past human anatomy. In her lap were a large canvas bag and some sort of stamped metal machine gun from over a century ago.

Over the roar of the bike and the whipping wind, the whine of a siren could be heard from behind them. His head whipped around in search of its source. Two box-bodied, black and white police cruisers with near ancient bubble lights spinning like tops above them. The cars themselves thrummed along with the siren. They pulsed in an impossible as if they were a massive organ, not a machine.

His partner beside him turned around and let a burst go from her weapon that sent spiderwebs through one of the cop's windshields and their car careening into the ditch alongside the desert road. Without a thought, he spun and let loose with a government-issued semi-auto as the remaining cop car sped as if to run them off the road. The recoil flew like lightening up his outstretched arm.

A beautiful grouping showed up as ragged glass holes above the cops' steering wheel. Slowly, tellingly, the car sputtered and slowed to a crawled to the edge of the road.

"Woo, baby, come give me another one!" he heard above the chaos in a sweet southern drawl. He obediently leaned over and planted another one on his ladies, vibrant lips. When doing so, the bike shifted just ever so slightly into the other lane. in time to meet an oncoming semi who barely had time to lay on his horn while cresting a hill.

Carter fell back, panting with a cold sweat breaking out on his skin. A kind of static energy stretched out from his chest.

'What!" he yelled.

He was on the roof in morocco. Kahina was there leaning over him, her chest heaving. Around her were fleeting pinpoints of light that would leave streaks in their passing. The entire air carried a bright sensation of firelight that pervaded his whole vision.

"Arlo... his name was Arlo Rodriquez, and her name was Delilah," she said excitedly.

Arlo? Yes, the man on the motorcycle was Arlo Rodriquez, and the woman was Delilah Hepburn. They'd robbed a bank in the southwest somewhere around the late 1950s, hoping to become the next Bonnie and Clyde. When Carter pushed, he could recall Arlo's memories as if they were his own. "Okay.... That's something I haven't seen, but." Carter began. Kahina moved towards him. Her hands ran up his torso pulling his shirt free from where it was tucked.

"You remember the first time they met? The first time they had sex?"

Of course, he did. They were the same night—a seedy motel just outside of her college town that Arlo was passing through.

"Yes." He said breathlessly while her hands traced up his stomach and began undoing the buttons of his shirt.

She looked him full in the face. Her eyes were bright with importance as she asked her next question.

"How does that make you feel? How do you feel about me, Carter?" The words burst from him so quick he could hardly stop them.

"We'll I Lo...." He locked his jaw tight to choke on the proclamation. His head was swimming with confusion at what had driven him to those words. Was it so simple? He thought. It was the drugs that were talking. Kahina spoke up, interrupted this line of thinking.

"Stop thinking like that! Just say it; it's not the drugs. Well, it's not just them. You didn't feel that way before the kiss, did you?" He stammered.

"No…no." even he could tell he was unsure of his doubts.

At this point, she'd worked far enough to have unbuttoned the whole shirt, even pulled herself on top of him. Her face was moving by his neck, up to his chin.

"Those emotions aren't fake, but they are new. Your mind is changing, Carter. OUR minds are changing."

He scoffed, gaining a bit of his composure.

"Lust, Kahina. drug-addled lust." He said, laughing. She'd pulled herself up until she was at eye level and murmured.

"Well, that is the first sign of it." Then bringing her face closer to his.

"Again," she whispered, sending shivers through his skin and down to his very bones.

Once more, her lips found him, and he pulled her into him until he felt himself sinking into the couch.

Then he opened his eyes to a new scene.

Small hands, both soft and dark, were grinding a green crown into a coloring book depicting an alpine scene of trees, mountains, and a bear cub following its mother down a forest trail. Looking up, it became apparent he wasn't alone on his little slice of domestic shag carpet. Opposite him was a small girl similarly dark-skinned, with two large puffs of hair beside her round doll-like face. She, too, was scribbling away at a coloring book as well. However, her weapon of choice seemed to be yellow.

The rest of the room was a technicolor delirium that dripped and melted in some places along the retro walls. Avant-Garde furniture seemed to stretch as if it was made of some elastic pulled across an axis. He was five years old, no six. He just had his birthday the week prior. His dad had bought him a BB gun with real scope, and his little sister Sadie, the girl opposite him, furiously coloring what seemed to be a sun, had started crying when she'd dumped fruit punch down her shirt. His name was Cory Levante.

A heavy-handed knock on the door sounded. He perked up at the sound.

"Just a moment!" a sing-song voice declared from the kitchen to his left. Shortly his mother walked through the doorway separating the living room and the kitchen making her way to the door. She was a tall woman with a proud face. Right now, she was sporting long braids, a lovely yet straightforward mandarin colored dress, and matching flats that stood out starkly against her skin. As she walked, she seemed to leave a trail of herself floating across the living room. A surreal progression that faded as Cory blinked,

His mother pulled the door open with a bright smile on her face that froze in confusion at what met her. Cory left his coloring behind and walked around the couch to better see the scene

Beyond his mother, two men stood near each other in dark fall coats. They seemed to blend like a dark pair fs Siamese twins. Softly, ever so softly, one of them said in the most somber of tones.

"Ma'am, there's been an incident at the factory."
His dad worked at a factory. This summer, they'd had a
family day, and he got to see a robot arm putting together
an airplane engine.

"We just need you to answer a few questions.
Mind if we come inside?" the other man asked.

His mother turned with a startling panic in her widening
eyes that made Cory's heart fluttered. He'd never seen that
before.

"Cory, baby. Take Sadie and go upstairs for a few
moments." She pleaded.

Cory nodded obediently and roused the oblivious
Sadie to gather their books and crayons and climb to his
room.

Once Sadie was settled and focused back in on her
rendition of a colorful beach, a dreadful curiosity
overcame him and made coloring seem rather dull.
Something bad was happening. Those men had told his
mother some bad news. Some secret news about his dad.

Slowly he got up from the forest scene he'd been
inscribing with color and crept from the room to the hall.
He stepped softly in his socked feet until he came to the
stairs. Then he moved every so silently down the first step,
then the second until he could see and hear the goings-on
below. At six years old, questions of national security
make no sense. The Agency badges and titles meant little.
Unfortunately, for his innocence, the only word that he
could find some context for in this sad short conversation
was the word suicide.

Out of all, this confusion rose a screaming sadness
that drowned out his capacity for any other thought. He

pulled his knees to his chest and buried his face in his folded arms, undertaking a doomed effort not to cry. Heaping warm tears soon ran amuck down his face. While he'd held in the sobs, he didn't hear the door shut, or his mother start up the stairs. It wasn't until she was a step away from him that he brought himself out of his shrinking world.

At first, Cory was sure she'd be mad at him for listening to the adults in secret, but when he saw a matching set of tears streaking her face, he let the sobs come to him. They sent big racking shivers down his body that made his stomach hurt and his head dizzy. He thought his bones might shake loose until she fell around him; engulfed him in her sobbing embrace. Finally, he gained the ability to form words in between each sob. It seemed the only one that would come through.

"Why?"

But his mother had no answer. She only pulled him tighter and planted a kiss on his forehead.

He blinked.

The mother was gone, and it was Kahina's lips on his forehead.

She eased back until she was sitting upright on his lap. She was crying just as the mother had been. He propped himself up on his elbow. Once he'd done that, she reached forward with both hands framing his face and wiped tears from his eyes with her thumbs. He was crying too, just as Cory had been.

"Her name was Jaquelyn." She said softly, dropping her hands from her face. Every movement of her arms seemed to send perceivable ripples through the space around them.

"I, I don't understand, are those real?" he asked, confused and breathless. Once more, he could remember that little boy's entire life. Only he had experienced what no little black boy in the American 60s would've.no Jim Crow, no civil rights failures. Hell, honestly, he'd say he couldn't even remember an example of segregation except that he also couldn't remember any white people either. History seemed to have different rules and events, maybe.

She smiled and shrugged as the last smear of someone else's melancholy was wiped away.

"I cannot say, Carter, I am a scientist, not a mystic. But the original plant I derived this from was said to give 'a hundred lifetimes of wisdom.' It was given to the matriarchs and shamans of an old tribe; whose practices predate the first wave of Islamists here."

He closed his eyes and shook his head. Wrong choice Carter. He felt an overwhelming wave of dizziness.

"Why, are you showing me this?" he asked, resting his head back on the couch cushions. His mind seemed to swim through three childhoods, and it was hard to tell where his original one ended and these two new inductions began. Everything was overlapping. He felt a stirring, really a warm grinding sensation against his groin. He opened his eyes to see Kahina's hips undulating over his own. Her smooth bare legs tightened on either side of him, each of her fingers pointed at her temples, and her eyes fluttered as she spoke.   "We are both nature and nurture, Carter. what our brain picks up as we grow it locks away in a fleshy little puzzle box." She dropped one of the accusatory fingers to his forehead and tapped.

"This helps unravel that puzzle."

"Clinical trials of my Tetowan capsules in patients suffering from over 25 different mental health disorders showed a 60% increase in receptiveness to psychotherapy when compared against control groups." She slowed the rotation of her hips until coming to a grinding halt. She stared out, northward over the city into the darkening distance, with a look of disgust that was frightening; the distortions he was experiencing made her scowl look feral and savage.

"But the Centrists have little need of such things, would they?" she muttered.

He could feel a shivering rage emanate from her. He put two hands onto her hips to still her but found her not to be moving.

"Their science departments wanted me to turn everything over to a
Cinopherm lead team."

Cinopherm, a company from the east with ties to the earliest
days of
centrism. Carter had seen their testing sights in the amazon. He'd guarded them, and he'd put them to the torch deservingly.

"I refused, and it was no small scandal; I'm sure I'd have been in more danger if they'd known I'd discovered their intent." She said.

A cold, sluggish sensation started up his spine.

"What, what could they want with this?" he asked, watching without complaint as she took one of his hands and brought It up to rest her face in it. He could still feel the warmth and moisture left by Jaquelyn's tears.

"They want to test and retool it as a reconditioning agent. I think their goal is to give it to children of the dissenting population." She said with a bare and horrifying agony. It made sense. The threat of generational insurrection had stymied much of the centrists' advances in some territories that wouldn't merely accept the double-edged sword that was centrist "Progress." With this, they could invade en-force with happy coalitions that bombed their way until nothing but a nation of orphans was left. Their schools could then feed them a diet of psychotropic pills and victor written histories to be taken as gospel. Anyone in a state like this would be especially…receptive…to suggestion.

His comforting hand flared to violent life near her face. It drove a vice-like grip into her slender neck and began to squeeze.

"You're just brainwashing me the same as they would!" Carter roared. He expected her to fight back, maybe even scream for help. He expected her to try and argue or defend her position with some moral high ground. Instead, she slowly nodded as another pair of tears rolled from her eyes.

His hand dropped limply to his lap, and she fell against him, heaving. Her warm breath seemed to match his chest's violent thumping. Slowly, ever so slowly, her form snaked up until she was cupping his face and tilting his head so that his ear was aimed at her lips.

"I am brainwashing you," she cooed. "But I am being brainwashed
right along with you. My dear, that is what love is."

"But why?" he asked.

She laughed pleasantly in his ear, and the sound seemed to echo back from somewhere in him, driving a dissonance between his ears and the world they tried to capture.

"You question everything. Good or bad." She said before biting his ear. she gave it a gentle tug with her teeth.

"I admired your work. I admire you. I want to see everything you're capable of." She pulled his hand up to her neck again. Forcing him to grip it. He followed suit, squeezing until she gasped. When her lips parted, he dove into them with his own.

Another life followed.

Eyes adjust from the dark into a hazy brightness. Bright light abounded and forced eyelids to flutter as everything came into focus.

Before these eyes were laid, a New England beach bathed in vanilla hues, to either side stretched this pale blonde sliver framed by grey boulders and towering alpines that caught a sea breeze. Like a dazzling starscape, each grain of sand caught the light in the most spectacular fashion. So much so that the eyes almost never looked nearer the body.

A set of slender pale hands poked out of a sweatshirt several sizes oversized for a small, feminine frame. In the right hand was a wet paintbrush held by fingers tipped by chipped pastel nails. The left had a palette whose smears of colors seemed to be endlessly spinning, self-contained whirlpools that were hypnotic in their simplicity.

These two instruments' subject was a half-plastered easel and canvas depicting the shoreline and at its center stood a trio of smooth, oblong stones stacked end to end impossibly. In reality, no such stones stood before her, and she seemed to conjure these from memory.

Her.

Yes her. Her name was June Pickett.

She'd gotten to pick that name not long ago. She supposed she could pick another surname as well while she was at it.

But for now, the throbbing watercolor in front of her was all that mattered.

"How's it coming, my dear!" came a call from behind her. She spun her head and felt with no small pride, her hair flip around from the movement. She was so proud of how long it had gotten; it made her feel so pretty even on days like this. The speaker was the most handsome man she'd ever seen strolling to her from the dunes.

A soft face despite its lines. That held a quiet, calm dignity so unlike the raucous boys of her hometown. Dark hair streaked with grey streamed from the top of his head in tight curls and continued down the sides of his face into a neatly trimmed beard.

Yosef Feidor strolled toward her in his full-length peacoat and a soft grey sweater with his hands tucked into the pockets of his slacks. An inexplicable mist seemed to pour off him, which June ignored in a dreamlike fashion. Even the fact that it would twist into tortured faces seemed to mean little only her dismissal of it seemed to stand out, but even that was put to the side when he spoke again.

"My, my, I'd say it's nearly finished." His eastern European accent only hung on at the end of his sentences, and she found it ever so enchanting. With a few more steps, he'd come behind her and wrapped his arms around her.

She laughed and winced as the noise escaped her. The sound was still not as feminine as she would like it to be. But his arms stayed, so she continued to speak.

"Hardly, I've probably got another hour or two before the sun goes down. I'd like to keep working." He held her tighter as a cold wind came from the ocean. She supposed it was strange her being with him. A twenty-year age difference would raise eyebrows. Then again, she concluded any man who chose her knew that was a choice that would raise eyebrows, so such thoughts were few and fleeting where Yosef was concerned.

"Oh, my dear, you'll be cold as ice by then."

"Yosef, I'll be fine, you worry to mu…." She couldn't complete the sentence.

Without warning, his hand closed her windpipe, and she was fighting for air.

"No, Thomas… I don't worry at all," he growled in her ear. That name! Why was he using that name! She didn't know what was happening. She fought to make words. Popping and straining lit up her neck.

"Yosef… why? Stop!" she croaked. She was slammed to the sand with one arm, and try as she did to fight and claw, she couldn't muster the strength to break his grip.

"All you little cretins." He was snarling and mad she'd never seen him like this.

"You are an abomination!" he roared into her face, and suddenly, a white-hot pain tore into her stomach and began traveling, ripping up her torso. Her vision tunneled and spun but stayed on his sweating face grimacing. The look was uncanny, like a poorly done wax dummy. The look she'd seen over her when they made love. In the end, the ecstasy showed through to be nothing more than confused anguish. With whatever time she had left, she tried to scrape together some understanding.

"You're free. You're free…free." He kept repeating, "Thomas, you are free." Where the last words she heard before she bled to death on those new England sands on a cold afternoon.

Carter gasped back to life in a panic pushing Kahina off him and the couch. His hands searched his body, his stomach but everything was intact. He was Carter; He was on a roof in morocco. He raised a shaking hand to his head and pulled his feet closer until he was nearly curled up on the couch.

"Fuck, how long does this last." He cried out with a sinking fear.

She rose unphased and brushed herself off before turning to look at the small bit of sunlight still playing with an ink colored sky. Maybe another half hour like this. After effects will last until the early morning." "That last one was…" he said, thinking back to horrors he'd never seen before. A whole host of untouched childhood traumas culminating in a violent helpless end. He'd never felt anything like it. In war, the violence didn't leave you a victim, only a hollow player. No matter how invested you made yourself; it wasn't the same. This had been so profoundly personal; this had been… his thought trailed off, and as he looked at Kahina's form with a new fear that was reaching a boiling point of horror.

As if feeling his gaze, she spun back to face him.

"Strong? Scary? I'd agree with you." She said, taking a few steps toward him before reading his demeanor.

"Are you okay?" she asked. The empathy was there, but it barely punched through his swirling fears. He shook his head.

"What does this mean? What does it all mean?" His voice cracked and without any warning, tears rolled from his eyes. She rushed to him, and although he wanted to pull back, he wouldn't let himself.

"Carter, Darling, I cannot rightly say." She said while running her fingers running through his straw-colored hair. "The old matrons say they are simply lessons, and this is simply a strong dose. There is no proof of it as having happened; it's just our subconscious minds playing off each other's stimuli until some stream of thought comes from it."

He shook his head forcefully before batting her hands away and pushing himself to his feet. He strode to the railing to overlook the town.

"No, that was real, I…June died and I could feel it."

"Just like I could feel the blood of the other seven girls he'd killed before her. Just like how I remember his parents being Judenrat during the holocaust or what the back of his drunken father's hand felt like, but they are just lessons," she said, then added as she neared him.

"Think about the painting. Was anything odd?" for a moment, Carter dug through the memories he now bore without asking for them. The sea, the stones... the moons.

"Two moons." He whispered before looking up and about the sky until he spun to see a far-off moon had already made its appearance. Only one of them, though, solitary in its pursuit of the sun. Yet, in every nighttime memory, June had always seen two. Kahina embraced him, her arms wrapping around his middle and pulling him close.

"These visions. I do not know what they are. I gave them power more than they ever had on their own. We have a daunting task ahead of us, my dear. But I want to face it with you, and these visions will help."

Her words stirred him to look down into a smiling face. The drug still played hell with his vision. Her skin seemed to move in unnatural ways, and parts of the face ebbed and flowed when no such movement should exist, but there was beauty there like he had never seen and familiarity that pervaded anything he knew.

"And these visions," she said, rising up on her tiptoes while his arms tightened around her. "We will face them together too." And they did.

The last of that afternoon was spent tangled in each other and another dozen or so glimpses into other lives, other worlds, neither knowing if they were real or ever glimpsed back at them. When all was said and done, they lay in a bare embrace watching the encroaching stars begin to peek through the final, bloody tempera of the sunset. With them now rested the memories of people who may or may not have lived, who may or may not have loved. Just as the memory of that day's sun.

Kahina's hand drew concentric circles upon his broad chest, and she smiled.

"I was a cold little girl. Very Distant." She said, her voice startled both of them as they could hardly remember how long it had been since either had spoken.

"The people around me meant little. It always drove my mother wild and broke the hearts of more than a few boys." Her eyes were lost in remembrance, and the circles her fingers drew. Then her circles stopped, and she folded her hands over her chest, making a small pedestal for her head to rest upon while she stared at him.

"But, I learned something tonight." She declared confidently. He looked down into her eyes, now made darker by the fading light. "And what is that?" Carter asked, brushing one hand over the side of her upturned head.

"That I love you, Carter Burke." He wanted to say it back. Right then, he wanted to lift her to the sky and yell it loud enough that it would carry across the bay to the scenes of carnage he'd left behind.

But he didn't get the chance. Fire and force ripped through the city, silencing any more topics of love that night.

Unbeknownst to them, the centrists had a nefarious plan in motion but a quarter-mile away from the pair. The EASP hydrogen fuel cells housed in tunnels below the complex had been rigged to blow in a spectacular false flag. This would create mass carnage that would ruin almost half the city in an apocalyptic explosion. There were hopes in the Centrist think tanks that always did their thinking far from public opinion. This would galvanize the European sector into a warlike attitude aimed at the barbarians beneath them.

In all this political positioning, over a hundred thousand would be considered dead or missing. In the end, Kahina and Carter's deaths were, as far as the authorities were concerned, just two more deaths that afternoon.

FIGHTING FAUST AND FURTHERMORE OTHER FIGMENTS OF FOLKLORE

"You play a pretty good fiddle boy but give the Devil his due."- Charley Daniels

<u>Prophecy</u> I

remember that it

hurt.

But I'd suffered no injury.

This memory was a self-made prophecy.

To fight it is to fulfill it.

Vulture

Your cultures are stillborn. They have been, from the start.

I grow stronger with each bite I pull from their
neonatal stories of self-importance.

Black wings will take the flight and I will circle the
next until I am full.

Horror in Motion

Step alone and lively no matter who's beside me.

I've a hollowed chest nothing escapes, nothing finds rest.

I lurch lustful and hungry.

My head one blurred memory of everyone who's fucked me.

I creep amidst confusion,

My identity shattered to a thousand slivers that reflect before they rend flesh.

DUST

After your deeds are forgotten, after the last echoes of the words you spoke are stifled, even your monuments will fall.

Fall to dust and be trampled by conquests of what beings come next.

In conciliation, even the stars are not eternal, and all will turn to darkness and dust.

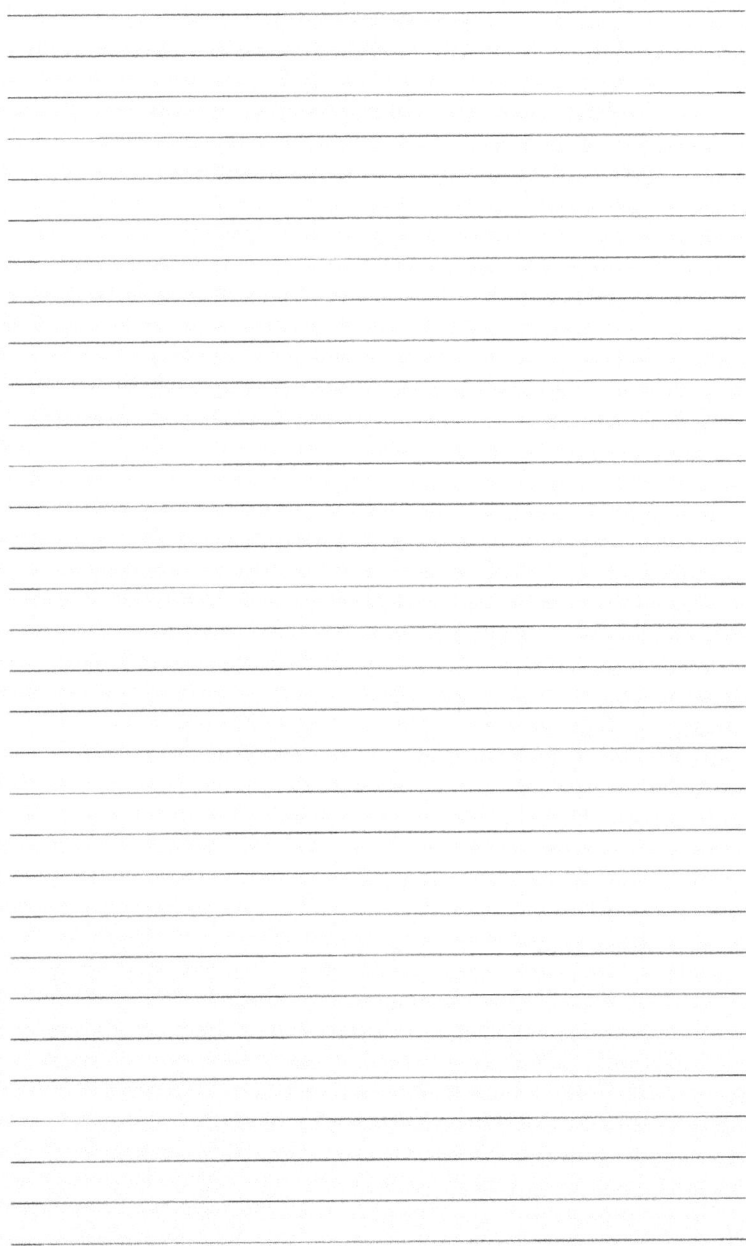

__Ghoul__

Yellow teeth crack scabs free with a lust to bleed.

Bring me fever, bring me pus, and bring me a lust

to be, I am pestilence and gluttony.

Beyond Based Beast

Kill me, burn me I'm a walking disease.

Fiend

I am no king,

My blood flows only with the fire to burn down empires.

This legacy will not be to build but to turn thrones to splinters.

Your hope should be that my children learn charity, or yours will starve in the rubble of what you've built.

Baptism

I'll keep a finger on the pulse of this world,

       Feel it flutter under bated breath.

Press until the blood wells up to the nail bed now vile intentions sit right at the fingertips.

Let me drown in them.

Call it a sanguine baptism painting my last breath in iron hues.

<u>Currents</u>

What becomes of all this stymied anger?
When a roaring current of friction surges for between myself?
When the universe meets the very dams it has emplaced? It's as though I'm left to drown or tread in my own hate.

But what a half assed lie that is. The universe, no more built the damn, than it gave any notion between myself and it.

Playing the victim seems to be my second favorite past time. It is eclipsed only by how I adore playing the perpetrator.

I sit in silent frothing madness as a slothful demon bears down on me.

I scream and call him temporary, but he chortles back with ease.

"you've left your pain behind now you're left with me."

A healthy life begets a mild mind as I smoothed its sharpest folds.

So, blank pages stand with headstone stillness and while cheap, slutty thrills promise fulfillment.

The calling

3 am, melatonin peak but still I'm denied sleep.

Should I call a pastor or a priest as a late-night fiend begins to creep?

I used to think it was because of witches, demons, or the ghosts of past heathens.

But as the hour draws to a close and no ghoul has been shown, I know the truth and the reason.

The devil won't sleep when there is work yet to do.

I won't rest until it's seen through.

OMEN

A black sheep sits with foaming lips dripping sick
from a peaking ram's head.

Ebon horns curl to crown a mindless god with belief
in nothing.

Eyes cut inhuman shapes and see inverted shades of
this life while truth flees him each night.

Hooves stamp hellbrands into foreign lands that
stretch on in a world alien to him.

Hunger haunts the hills while he jaunts past maws
that beg for substance.

He is paid mind only by shamans, magic men, and a
few bleeding women of gypsy suspicion

He's a bad omen to all of them.

Wrath

Black eyes peer back from a sneering mirror of myself.

A reflected perception shows my true intentions.

These black eyes flinch at any kindness but drink up the 24-hour cycle of violence.

They watch me scream and snarl with no want of victory since right or wrong don't mean shit to me.

COLLOQUIM

Mr. West is sitting alone in some dark corner booth of a bar. This establishment is so alike all the others he's frequented across this spinning rock that it seems to spring to life purely from a state of frozen memory rather than the material world. The only real difference in this re-ran episode of personal destruction is that he would typically find himself saddled up to the bar. His favorite pastime has always been making fleeting friends with other despicable drunks so that he can stave off the choking loneliness of yet another solo trip to the bar.

Let's take a closer look and see if we can get to the bottom of whatever has driven him to further isolation. Yes, yes, the regular glass of midprice scotch on the rocks that leaves a smoky taste in the back of his throat. Nothing new there. But what's this? It seems he isn't truly alone. How'd we miss such a thing? Across the table is a sharp dressed man of middle age in a sleek black suit minus the tie and vest. He stares at the younger man with an undefinable look of enraptured disinterest before he speaks up with a dusky drawl that shakes Mr. West from his whiskey trance.

"Well, Mr. West, I say it's about time

we begin." Mr. West nods, not making eye

contact.

"You can call me Rob, you know, or Tristen, or Bobby, if you'd
like.
I mean hell, I guess you rate to call me doc."

The words come out sheepishly and an awkward chuckle punctuates them in an attempt at familiarity that seems to fall deadpan on the man across the table.

"This is a formal matter, Mr. West, so we will be using your formal name."

Once more, Mr. West nods, falling back to his gridlock stare on the amber glass before him that is slowly sweating poison onto a bar coaster. The man across the table shuffles a sheaf of papers that may or may not have been there just a glance ago.

"Now, your request is quite a peculiar one. It's normal to be asking for fame, or money, some form of power and prestige, but this..." he says as he gives the papers a tap with a twisted ashen finger.

Something patronizing in his tone seemed to stir some fire in Mr. West. He finally looks the other dead in the face. In his own mind, he tells himself the unease rising in his gut is simply the mix of liquors that lead him here.

"Really? It shouldn't be peculiar at all. It hasn't been that long since Faust has it? Do you forget so easily?" he sneers.

A frown tugs at the corner of the other man's lips but for a moment, but that moment is enough to bolster our young Mr. West into a smirk.

"You've found some steel for your voice there, did you? Or is that just you yelping at the whip of insecurity biting your back?" the sentence had tapered into a low growl that brought beads of sweat streaming down Mr. West's neck.

His only response is to maintain his glare and knock back another mouthful of scotch. It seems he is pouring effort into the hope that if he blacks out later, he could erase the Other's dark eyes from his memory.

"Moving on, let's review your terms; if you can call them that." He looks at the papers and gives a sickening chuckle that could crumble graves to dust. "To simply be happy?" he then points to the bar.

"Go be happy for the night, don't bother me with some trivial tantrum that you've spun up."

Mr. West's gaze follows his finger to see a group of women looking good enough to hold his attention on any other night but this one.

"I said happy, that's just feeding a hunger." He says and drains the last of his glass in one big gulp.

"Is that any different?" The man across the table says, gesturing to the empty glass resting once more.

"Touché." Mr. West says flippantly. A moment of heavy silence passes between the two until Mr. West speaks again.

"I'm tired of feeling this; I'm tired of being this." He pleads. If the other man cared for the desperation, then he showed no sign.

"What could you give me for this? You're nothing but a spectacle. you'd be an advertisement, I suppose."

Mr. West nods

"I suppose I could."

The other's Smug silence seems to be an answer itself, so He lets out a sigh.

"And what good is that? In a world like this"

"No matter. In any case, I should be honest with you, Mr. West, I simply cannot accept this offer."

In a bare-faced fit, Mr. West slams his fist down on the table and lets loose his own growl.

"And why the hell can't you?"

"Any number of reasons, my dear boy, but why on earth do you want this?"

He scoffs

"Because I deserve it! I deserve to be happy."

"Despite your sins?"

"Because of them!" he lashes back.

The other wags a finger at him.

"Melodrama won't get you anywhere, Mr. West other than being kicked out of here."

His bit of prophecy comes true shortly as a waitress nears the booth holding a check he hadn't asked for just yet.

"Hi, sir. We have your check here. The manager wanted us to go ahead and uh, give it to you."

Mr. West rubs his face before donning a disheveled look of understanding before speaking again.

"Cut off, huh?" he asks her, but our distraught bastard already knows the answer, doesn't he?

The waitress simply adopts a thin-lipped smile in a look of patronizing regret at her position in this and gives a little nod.

The other lets out a laugh.

"Time for us to move along, Mr. West."

He says.

"So, what is this happiness you deserve?"

The other asks after they've found a more hospitable environment in an alley beside the bar. The only companies the two have are the uniform green dumpsters and sterling trashcans that live here between the lazily painted brick edifices that line the alley walls. Farther up, a mysterious pipe or seldom-used fire escape might also stand a gargoyles vigil, but our focus is on subjects not nearly as lofty.

Mr. West, who is bracing himself against the wall with one hand and furiously plumbing the back of his throat with the other, is dry heaving over a spattered heap of bile and whatever dinner he had. Looking down, we can see; some contemporary art piece born from the top floor of his bowls rather than his heart. A few droplets have fallen astray to his scarred boots that once upon a time was expensive and fashionable, at least for him. Luckily, it seems none of it has soaked the fabric of his pants

"You said We couldn't deal." He says, all bleary-eyed and haggard from another bout of alcoholic bulimia, "Why are you hanging around?"

"You wanted to deal." He says, "So, we'll deal until we're done."

Mr. West let out a tired sigh that dripped a string of bile and spits that he wipes away with a green sweater sleeve before turning to the Other.

"Well, what do you want?" he asks him. Only to hear the same question from a moment ago.

"What is this happiness you deserve?" the Other reiterates. Only this time, he adds.

"What does it mean to you?" The other draws near to his red-eyed subject with a rotten, toothy smile rooted on his wrinkled face. Mr. West begins stammering. He's apparently trying to articulate something, but he can't seem to find the words before gripping the sides of his head as if experiencing a splitting headache or some acute form of anguish.

"Pathetic." The Other spits out, "You don't even know what it is you're asking for, do you? What kind of place does that leave us, Mr. West?" The young man slumps against a trash can and hangs his head low. "Guess you've got the reigns." He says sullenly, unable to meet the Other's eyes.

"I always had them; that's the problem. Now come on."

At the curb just outside the alley sits a dark muscle car that may or may not have been there originally. Its make and model you can't be sure. Only that it is a classic, and a meticulous set of hands has performed its upkeep. Sleek, shimmering, and black from the metal of the body to the tint of the glass. The Other is walking towards it. Reluctantly, with a final look around the destitute alleyway, Mr. West begins to follow. He opens the passenger side door as the other settles into the driver seat. Before Mr. West can drop into the passenger side, the seat flips forward, activated by some unseen lever.

"In the back, Mr. West. I do insist." And wouldn't you know it? The young man follows suit. There he goes clambering ^{into}   "Mr. West, If that is truly your desire…" he is cut off by the rising anger of the ward he has undertaken.

"Well, what other destination could there be!" he roars in a still buzzing rage.

Dark, hideous laughter begins to come from the other's turned away
face. It's a sickly sound that has all the lure of a pneumonia patient dislodging phlegm. Soon, this sound rumbles into silence, giving way to his disquieting voice, a welcome intrusion by comparison.

"Now, Mr. West, for someone in your profession, you must learn to be more careful with your words."

He scoffs again.

"It's not a profession; it's an obsession." He mumbles with crossed arms. The brakes are slammed, Tires screech against an unseen road and Mr. West is catapulted into the back of the seat in front of him.

Before he can entirely right himself, the other is leaning over him with a foul snarl that makes a rubbery mask of his too wrinkled face. Twin sets of teeth sit in his mouth like rows the back seat, finding only black leather and a sense of spinetingling Déjà vu. The interior of the car is soundless to a deafening degree. Every heartbeat and wayward thought seem to scream in the silence. Even the other turning the key in the ignition does nothing to flood the space with the customary sound of a purring engine. This all leaves our intrepid little dipshit fidgeting nervously, waiting for the Other to finally speak.

"You aren't going to throw up in my back seat, are you?" he asks in a tone that isn't denoting any degree of good humor.

Mr. West laughs this off.

"I haven't decided yet." He jests, raising no laughter from his driver. The other's eyes are affixed on whatever rests outside the windshield. What that is isn't truly discernable at the moment. Sure, the headlights go out, but they fall on nothing as if they are carving empty space free of a void.   "Where are we going, Mr. West?" he asks with the passing concern of a chauffeur who gets his wage no matter the destination. Mr. West sits in the dubious confusion that seems to be his theme tonight.

"I'm not sure I follow." He speaks, his voice catching in his throat. The mystery of what was beyond that windshield struck him. Not in the way of staring down an unnamable horror but an indescribable terror that drives thrillseekers to euphoria.

"You aren't following that is correct." The driver says. His gnarled hands wrap like perched talons at a deliberate ten and two on the wheel. For what reason is hard to discern as there are no perceivable curves on this nonexistent road.

"You are being driven, Mr. West. now decide where." He orders as if now there is some invisible cab fare is being run-up, and he'll be left footing the bill.

Mr. West scoffs.

"To madness."

The driver is having none of this. The young man's episode of pitiful angst seems a drab thing to him.

of dejected tombstones found in the forgotten cemeteries Mr. West had explored as a morbid boy. The eyes are coal dark and glimmering with an oil slick sheen as his words tear into the young man. They ramble forth with the clatter of those awful gnashing teeth and smacking of dry lips.

"So, you choose now to call upon me like you always do! When your mountainous ego is made frail, and you're tossed headlong into another fit of melancholy. It must fall to me to fix it! Am I overlooking any details, Mr. West?" he spits his name out like it's a mouthful of dust. In true hot-headed fashion, the young Mr. West opened his mouth to protest, to give some retort that would rally himself to his own defense.

But nothing comes forth. His own words have abandoned him, and why shouldn't they, when he'd been so negligent of the symbols that made humanity?

"Now, think for a moment of anything outside yourself if you can." The other continues. He's placated enough now to turn away from Mr. West with the car lurching forward once more in silent progress.

"Do you think I enjoy being at the beck and call of every talentless hack at the end of his rope? Think of how tired I must be of hearing eons of sob stories strewn together by failures scraping themselves off the floor."

He says this, of course, as Mr. West is righting himself from his dejected position occupying the floorboard.

"I'm…sorry?" He responds pensively, unsure of what the proper response should be in this case.

"No, you aren't, so, don't attempt to be. The only thing you are sorry for is that the world won't unravel itself and all it's mysterious before your tiny little mind." The other shakes his head.

"You are turning out to be just another dullard wanting to play the hero of his own story when he can't even realize one simple fact."

"And what fact is that?" Mr. West asks. "You don't get to write the setting. The setting writes to you." The other declares poignantly.

Mr. West shakes his head.

"No." he says firmly, "I don't accept your fact."

"And you do you intended to follow through on this denial

"Well, then." The Other says, "That is rather unheroic of you, isn't it?"

"Well, then maybe I'm not very heroic." He fires back.

"so, you say?"

"I wasn't very good at it anyway."

"In your own eyes, no. You seemed quite dreadful." The Other agrees.

"So, what should I be instead? Me?" he asks.

"Don't ask stupid questions. You'll be a version of yourself no matter what you do." The Other chastises, "Now let's think a bit more, extravagantly shall we?"

Without warning, a burning cigarette and a Fluted glass full of a bubbling drink sit in each of the young man's tattooed hands. He takes a sip and comes away with a quizzical look.

"What the fuck is in this?" He asks, finding it confusingly sweet but not distasteful.

"Oh, my apologies, wrong story." The other says with a knowing cackle meant only for him, and well...for you as well. The fluted glass is gone, and in its place is a half-full bottle of rye clutched by the neck.

"I…" Mr. West began before trailing off while he examined the familiar bottle.

"Poured that down the drain a few months back in some solo act of melodrama thinking it would cure your bad habits."

"Well, yes." He agrees.

"And what was the result?" the Other asks.

"I suppose I wasted good whiskey." Mr. West gravely proclaims, then takes a hearty pull.

"Now, back to the deal at hand, if you aren't a viable hero, then what should you make of yourself?"

"A villain?" he states simply before puffing on the cigarette.

"No! don't play dumb for my benefit. Your brain is grey matter through and through. I know you aren't so black and white."

"Hmm, an anti-hero?" he tries again only to be met with a haughty laugh from his driver.

"If you want to live out a dime-store pulp fiction novel, go right ahead." He says with a dismissive wave of his hand before returning it to the wheel.

"No, that wouldn't amount to much." Mr. West agrees after another smoky drag.

"So, dig a little deeper." He responds excitedly, hungrily even.

"Then, I'll be a pariah." The Young man says with equal excitement.

"Yes." The other practically hisses. "In the most classical sense."

Mr. West takes another swig then adopts a smirk that curves up the left side of his face in a devilish fashion before it falls flat again when he realizes they were stopped at the same street they'd left.

"What is this?" he asks the other.

"You never gave me a real destination, so here we are." The other says as the door opens and the passenger seat slides forward to let him out.

Mr. West sits there on the mysterious dark leather for another moment, not yet wanting to walk once more on the concrete sidewalk where he'd stand amongst the downtown buildings' silent and aging fronts.

"Come now. Mr. West, it's time you get a move on." Says the other, and for a moment, it seems like a somber inflection might be secretly riding his vile voice. Mr. West abides by this advice and crawls out of the back seat to find himself under a streetlight looking back into the black car, meeting the ethereal eyes inside that match it's glossy exterior.

"Remember, Pariahs, are at their root untouchable." The driver says his passing wisdom slowly, and Mr. West gives a determined nod.

"Wait." Mr. West pipes up. "What about the deal?" he asks. And just before the door shuts.

"I can't accept any deal with you, Mr. West. What did I just tell you?"

The car drifts off silently before disappearing around some distant turn Leaving us only with our intrepid, dipshit, pariah swaying to the beat of a sloshing whiskey bottle he lifts to his lips. When it's completely drained, he lets out a ragged breath that turns to a coughing laugh. He drops the bottle to the sidewalk, and just before he staggers into the night, he declares in a whisper that only we can hear.

"Untouchable."

War In The Catalyst

"..."

Settler

A short jaunt into the wilderness and I thought the journey done.

I'd settled into naivety as if it were my destination.

A Traveler may learn from the path beaten under feat but until learning turns to actions and hands grasp tools; nothing shall be changed but a traveler to a fool.

Man of Words

What's a man of words who isn't a man of his word?

A sideshow magician tricking kids into
mysticism or
A snake oil salesman who can't stomach his own
medicine.

So, I'll rage at that reflection and scrape my mantras
in my skin all in the hope; I don't forget myself again.

Firestorm

Guttering

Sputtering

Bed of coals

Menagerie of gleaming demons held on short

leashes A calm breeze blows an air of new

direction.

Now the chaff burns on the threshing floor.

Wildfires loom

My putrid cities shudder.

Afterbirth

One day I will write without pain; the creation will come without the flow of blood.

But any mother will tell me such things are lies of the highest degree, and Truth is what I seek.

Truth and life.

 Truth of life is that to live is to know strife.

 Truth in death is that death offers peace.

But such stillness offers little comfort to me.

"Self Help"

A hundred Billy Graham's of making a billion dollars,

Nothing new between their pages, just fake smiles spewing vagueness.

"Trust the process,"

I'll give you a new sermon kid.

"Trust the chaos,"

Don't run from the nights where you kill bottles and give into bar fights.

Eat the fear that cuts you free of love and find a passion beyond heartache and hate.

<u>Featherweight</u>

Bones turned yellow and lungs turned black with a soul to match.

All in orbit around a heart of gold.

I'll break that scale when my eyes touch the afterlife.

I'm just a Bible belt bastard
    born with an appetite for
        brimstone.
Always had an epitaph on my lips and fingertips for
every hellfire spark that licked my skin.

I've spent days under the desert sun, even swallowed
the jungle's heat and blown enough smoke to make
you think a worm lived in my throat.

This blood runs hot and this pulse rate spikes like a
drop of mercury racing to the top of Fahrenheits.

So, just know, no rain, no storm, and no snow.

    No natural state or human hate,

        Can turn this heart cold.

Heroes or Forefathers?

I can't call you either.

Whisper instead "We are kin" from the grave.

If my legend swells beyond your shadows; Just keep your coffins still and know brothers, the difference was always this.

My skull was suicide proof and yours was merely a magnet.

A New Path

I thought it was the chaos that kept me true to myself.

I'd hunted it with wild eyes and trigger pulls. Another taxidermied memory of wild nights and barley making it back pinned on the walls of a thing I called life.

But the chaos was never what built me. That was a family that longed for peace.

The chaos never saved me; that was my brothers and sisters with no blood ties who'd tie twisted knots in the lifelines I kept cutting.

All this time, I stood on the backs of angels and mistook the teeth of chaos for a tender kiss.

My affair with it is not over but I walk a new path and will hunt it longer and haunt it instead.

<u>Stand firm and bend no knee</u>, let your feet sink like
rooted trees.
Stand so tall when fear wears your face, you won't
see the mockery.

Stand ready, your troubles are only beginning.

The gods feared the titans, so you may grow to hate
your victory.

Is it blasphemy, to write a new reality or madness, to
divorce from this one?
In truth, I think it's the only way to save the humane
side of me.

We must ascend from this human condition or only
death will set us free

215

Inept Immortality

I'll know no
grave, No
mausoleum.

Turn my body into
relics, Let me haunt your
museums.

Build a throne of my bones,
Make my flesh a tapestry.

Hollow my skull into a chalice and toast on far
away planets.

Turn my memory to a martyr and lose all sense of
me, Exalt my soul into an idol and torch your
cities.

When my name is stricken, and my essence is
aether, I'll still stalk this place in the hearts of
rebels.

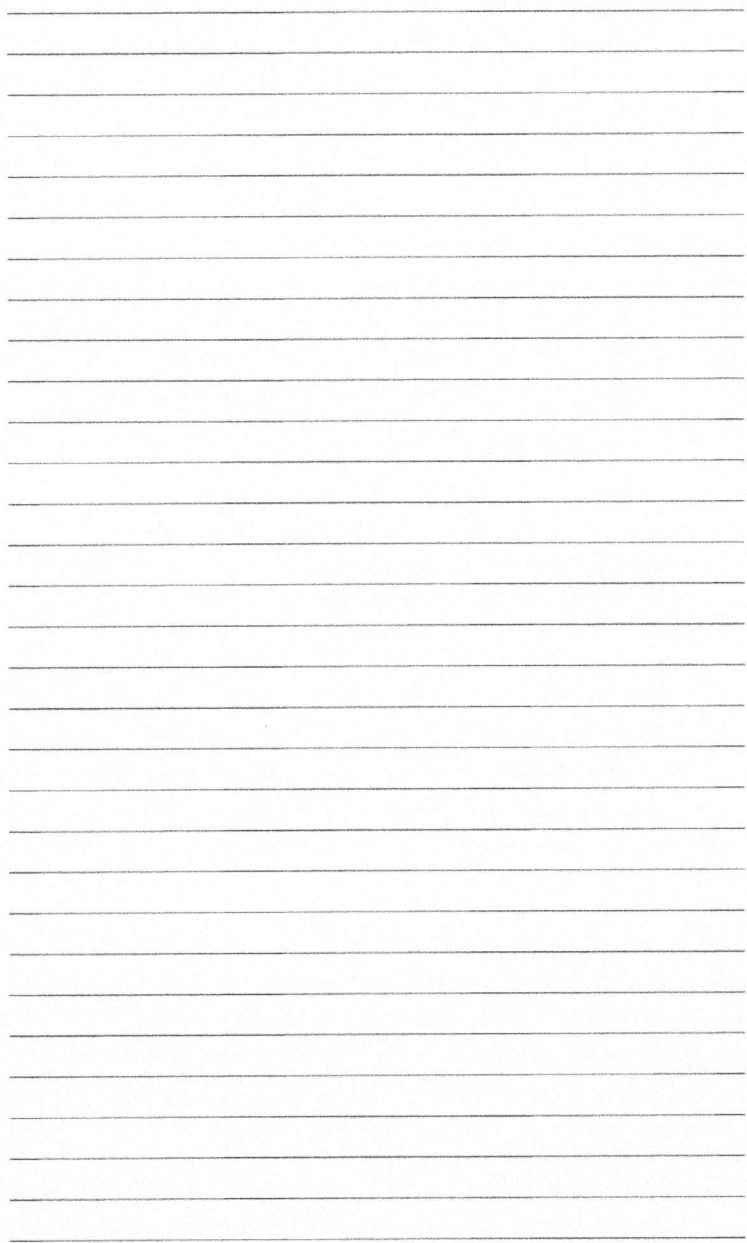

Recipe

Melt my mind to make a meal, suiting my appetite, the most absurd pallet since Hannibal gave us his narcissist lecture.

But listen, Clarice, listen this time it's a whole new craze!

As the days drain, the flesh is made tasteless there is a better way to season the brain.

It's tenderized by the daily beatings, but it's that marinade that has these grey folds singing.

Let stew in a slew of the absurd until mania is the prevailing flavor, and just when madness nears to take its licks remind it of its table manners.

Renewable Resource

There is nothing more plentiful than nothing, as nothing is all there is.

It's the mind that tries for something and gets tired of all of it.

The mind forgets it is nothing and nothing's more plentiful than that.

Revelations

Awake each day to a fresh apocalypse, lacking any biblical sense.

These hero and villain complexes fold and unfold as my world turns to ash. All while, new seeds bury themselves into ancient bones, only recently planted amid endless cataclysm.

Still, I learn Christlike forgiveness while I nurture old testament anger.

I come down from caves of allegory. I walk with the weight of a godless world.

Without him, I find the devil a myth and pack on the weight of my sins.

Giving in to these newsreels to night terrors, I'm met with cherub trumpet blasts until I strike blind my third eye and foster an antichrist to watch with me as the world dies.

SUICIDEPROOF

-I've bit it-

-The blue steel of a shotgun barrel-

-I've felt it-

-The cold scrape of metal on my palate-

-I've tasted it-

-The empty appetizer of a buckshot oblivion-

-Only saved by a safety I never flicked and left with an epiphany on my lips-

-I won't be the one to pull the trigger that does me in-

Sisyphus

This stone is mine and mine alone.

I dug it up; I've carved it out.

It's not a burden; it's my calling.

This hill I'll walk, and this boulder will roll with
me, still smiling.

Torchbearer I've feared that if this rage subsides my heart will wither and dry.

> What am I without this self-destruction?

> Creation and vision seem to stem only from the hadron collision in my mind.

> I've lived a life of fire and on fusion on the edge of combustion.

> Now I've gotta keep the flame alive while the rest dies.

Their Eyes

You're nothing more than a voice scratched hoarse
wishing to be seen.

Die in their eyes pass on to the next life.

See who rushes selfless towards the scene.

Way their actions against your strife.

Or don't, stay a bystander's dream.

Whose Villain?

In my soul, there is a hunger to conquer and control.

It sets my teeth to gnashing and my heart to wail and moan. I'll exhume these dark intentions of Machiavelli villain and stich him up a new visage.

With eldritch intentions I give this cadaver new life, new vision.

To be this worlds reaction, the evil which evil has begotten.

Call Him Nothing

Synapse snap back from the first look at any peace these grey folds have seen.

The Truth of The Void

Now, nothing gives way to the light. Stitching particle to particle until a single article can call on himself.

WHITE LIGHTER FULL OF PHEONIX FIRE

I can't remember who said it so it must have been me.

My own dark demon whispering while I sleep.

"Kid don't burn your lucky before sunrise…" But

luck is always on my side even when fortune is not.

So I'll play with black cats and break mirrors at a glance.

And when that moon won't shine and darkness pulls at a blue sky I'll fish it out my pocket and I'll crumble up the pack.

It's the last one standing and it's flipped on its head so when the white lighter kicks I'll just grin, that 27 club is gunna have to pencil me in.

Fuck off you don't get to take notes on that one.

EXALTED

It's an awkward thing coming to consciousness sitting on a park bench wearing a tattered, mud speckled three-piece. It's made even stranger when you didn't wake up like this. It wasn't some drunken string of misdeeds that had to lead him to sleep on the park bench. No, it was as if his brain had simply been turned off while his body was still moving. Until finally coming to this position, and now the switch had been flipped back to on. His mind might as well have been a telecast of static for all the thoughts he could assemble.

This left a substantial amount of unaccounted time on his hands— specifically, from birth to this moment. Not a single memory could be pulled from his scrambled mind, not even a name. Finally, a thought rose to the surface, wallets. Wallets carried ID and other little clues to who he was, how he got here, and maybe even what he should about those first two things.

It didn't take long for the plumbing of his pockets to prove fruitless.

Although, inside these empty palms were a series of intricate geometric tattoos. His eyes scanned the symmetrical dots and interwoven lines, examined them closely from left to right, and found them very similar in style but different patterns. He ran his fingers over them, feeling little scar tissue and seeing some fading on the smaller lines. It was clear these weren't a recent addition.

It seemed like there weren't many answers on his person. So, he took up a new approach. He surveyed his surroundings. It was a verdant park lush with greenery and devoid of people. Currently, he sat just off of a paved walking path on a dark bronze colored bench. To his left and right was a meticulous and unbroken line of elm trees whose intergrown canopies offered shade from the rising sun to the path and his bench. Beyond this was a field that, on some other day, would have been a perfect place for a picnic, but it seemed the caretakers had grown a little lax, and as a result, the grass was grown nearly to the height of his shins.

It was while he was sitting here taking in the greenery in the midmorning sun, he heard a commanding voice call out to his left.

"Sir, what are you doing out right now?" it asked with a sternness that could come only from often flexed authority.

He turned to look at the source and found two cops walking down the path. They each wore flat gray uniforms that seemed utilitarian in nature, large cargo pockets on the limbs, and lacking any frills. Over this, they had heavy black tactical vest sporting pouches and straps a plenty loaded down with who knew what. On their hips were belts with pistols, batons, and a can of mace the size of a small fire extinguisher, which he believed to be an excessive size. On their shins and forearms as well, they seemed to have some form of lightweight plastic guards as well.

While he was the only other person in sight, it still took a moment to register that he was the one being addressed. He sat stock-still unsure of what to do or why sitting on a park bench seemed to be a public offense.

"The city is still locked down, sir." The one on the right said. That one seemed a little younger, with a square face as opposed to his partner's drooping round one, but they both sported uniform crew cut brunette hair. "Do you live nearby? we can escort you home." The young one asked.

He stammered as he heard his voice for the first time. It sounded like a snake wielding Pentecostal sermon softened by an easy beach bum canter.

"I… I don't exactly uh, know…. Officer." he said with a grin, hoping that might keep things peaceful.

The two came within eight feet of him and rested with hands on their hips perched just a hairs length from the butts of their pistols.

The Older one let out an annoyed sigh.

"Alright, sir, then you're gonna have to come with us. Turn around and put your hands behind your back, please." And with that, the older officer began walking forward while fiddling with his belt for some handcuffs.

"Wait, please, you don't have to…" he started to say, raising his hands and shrinking into the bench. The cop didn't come to a single step closer. A sharp blast from behind the cop tore the officer's face apart in an explosion of meat and blood that showered over the seated man.

"FUCK!" he screamed as the cop hit the ground like a bundle of cordwood with brains leaking from his face to the grass.

Looking past the dead man, he saw the other cop black pistol raised with a determined look tightening his face before his eyes panned up, looking past the still leveled gun to that of the man on the bench. Once they met, he smiled with a euphoria that seemed out of place in the face of his act.

"I didn't believe it." The living officer said breathlessly. He dropped the pistol back into its holster and walked forward, stepping over his dead compatriot.

"Then, I saw your markings and knew it must be true." With that, he ceremoniously dropped to his knees and put his face in the dirt, bowing before the muddy, bloody, man without memories.

"I'm sorry. I don't understand." He pleaded nervously to the man before turning this way and that in a furious search to see if anyone else noticed the murder that occurred at his feet—there were no witnesses but the trees, and they wouldn't offer any help or hindrance.

The young cop rose to his knees and looked at him quizzically.

"You're the Exalted One." He said as if it was the most obvious thing in the world. "I am one of the children; it is so great that you have returned to us."

"Um, sir, I don't know what the hell you're talking about." He said as his shaking hand raised up to wipe the blood from his face. It only smeared it, so he pulled the cuff of his suit up to blot it out.

The confusion was plain on the young cop's face and he wore a disapproving frown that seemed menacing somehow. The man on the bench began thinking he might have made some errors and should slow down and think. Perhaps, it might have been better to just play along with whatever the guy who'd just turned his coworkers head into a fucking canoe had been saying.

"Then you have not come back to us." He finally said, "If you are still lost to us, perhaps this body before me has served its purpose." His grip on the pistol did not slacken.

Only a single word began rolling through his head on repeat as this psycho's cold eyes bored into his person.

Fuck.

He felt like he might clam up, vomit, shit himself, and take off sprinting into the field before him only to be gunned down by a murderous evangelist. Only he did none of those things. That Tv static he'd felt when coming to consciousness flooded out the panic, and his thoughts became lucid, and survival became a clear path.

He grinned and held his arms open with the palms facing out and grinned a soft, inviting smile.

"My child, you have done well. Not only are you devoted, but you know that no single body is more important than the collective Soul." He said in an eloquent voice flowing from somewhere other than the source of the shaky stammering he'd been struggling with earlier. What the fuck, he thought in his head absently, was 'the collective soul, ' although it didn't feel as though he was bullshitting on the spot. He could tell he was saying something of worth. Apparently, the cop thought so as well as his cold eyes lighted, and a joyous smile split his face. Hesitantly he moved forward to embrace the man on the bench who, in turn, enveloped the officer in his arms. After the short hug, the two split and the cop spoke again.

"I knew it; I knew you would not abandon the children. I will take you to them. You'll be safe!" he said excitedly. The man on the bench nodded stoically before standing. Then he said.

"A perfect plan. You are quite worthy of the blessings you shall receive." He said, holding his hands out to aid the officer in standing.

Shortly after, the cop was leading the memoryless man out of the park with him now wearing the protective vest of the dead man they'd left by the bench. Creeping panic was crawling up his neck. He knew little about this cult of violent fanatics he was apparently a figure in. Sure he'd spat some vapid bullshit out already that had landed thanks in no small amount to luck, but he knew that wouldn't keep him alive much longer. So, he started to prod a bit to see if he could learn anything else about this cult.

"Tell me, brother. What is your name," he asked the cop walking at his left. The man was taller than him, broad and well-built for a job that might have him wrestling the unwilling into cuffs.

"I am Dennis Knapp."

He responded monotonously but did not look to the other man. Instead, his eyes were busy. Though his face was locked forward, his eyes would dart to and from their midline in a kind of passive security sweep. The effect was robotic.

"And, how did you, Dennis, come to follow my teachings?"

This broke through the uncanniness that Dennis had been showcasing so eerily. His face brightened, caught inside a fond memory.

"Well, it was a little over three years ago, forgive me, I know time is of no importance, and I'd found myself in a horrible place. The woman I was with had cheated on me, and the police academy was hard on my body and mind. But, I found your videos and your story, and they uplifted me, and I no longer felt so alone." He said happily.

"I was only involved online in the forums until after I graduated and joined the city's force. But then I started going to the collections. It was there I saw the miracles of oneness and fully professed myself." He tapped the vest over his chest with the last one.

"I was marked and accepted into the collective soul connecting my spirit to all." He said proudly before adding

"I am ashamed Exalted one. I have not been able to accept any other markings, or I would lose my job and be considered an outlaw like the others." He said solemnly. The 'Exalted One' did not comment for a moment, and Dennis continued to speak.

"But, my position has allowed me to help many of the collected to safe places like the one I am taking you. Even if it slows my own exaltation for a time, I am welcome to help others stay safe at such times as these."

He said with renewed pride before finally breaking his forward gaze to look at the other man with hopes of praise in his eyes. The TV static wiggles its finger back into the mind of the 'Exalted One,' and he spoke softly like a parent to a child.

"It is well that you are willing to deny this self, Dennis, for such things, you will be rewarded."

Dennis was speechless. His sharp jaw hung slack, and it looked like tears welled up in his strange eyes.

"Thank you, exalted one. This has made me quite happy." He choked up on the last bit of the sentence before composing himself with a gruff cough and returning to his forward-facing march.

Leaving the park, the two of them came to what should have been a bustling downtown street. Instead, not a soul could be seen in either direction, and only a handful of seemingly abandoned vehicles sat at the feet of the grand skyscrapers. As the pair turned to walk down the sidewalk, he noticed piled mounds of parking tickets accumulated under their wipers. He may not know his real name, but he knew this wasn't the status quo.

"Dennis," the exalted one said, "I have been gone for some time... I have been... elsewhere preparing things. What has happened in my absence?"

"Well, after the incident in Portland, the entire collective began to be hunted by the governments of the world. Many of us were distraught, sure that the Lesser had gotten to you, Others lost faith completely. As well the incident caused many things: earthquakes, Tsunamis on all the coasts in the pacific. Then the Lesser lashed out again. It began killing indiscriminately, engulfing entire towns in the Midwest, and seemed to be making his way east towards us maybe. But since then, that has stopped."

Well, that didn't tell him shit about the vacant cars and empty streets. Maybe there was more that had gone wrong with the world before this mysterious 'incident.' Another curiosity he had from Dennis's statements was that upon the mention of the "Lesser," the passive static that had been ebbing and flowing in his mind kicked up like an angry swarm of bees for half a heartbeat before disappearing almost completely for a moment. But, by the time they had reached the police car parked on the corner of the street, they followed. It had crept its way back into his mind and resumed its passive presence.

"I see, well, Dennis, don't be disturbed. The Lesser shall be dealt with." The 'exalted one' said. However, he was unsure of what any of it really meant and feeling definitely disturbed by its connotations. Dennis just opened the rear car door and nodded along grimly.

"Inside here exalted one, I will get you there quickly." He said, motioning to the backseat. The exalted one complied and lowered himself into the metal caged car, feeling like a rat in a trap by the time the door closed. Soon, Dennis was at the wheel and driving. Little conversation was occurring due to the heavy plexiglass and steel barrier between the two. Instead, the exalted one watched out the window and tried to develop some greater understanding of where he was. It was while he was mulling over whether or not this was New York city or how he would even know if it was that his day got even stranger.

The Lesser is going to be a problem. You are right to be worried. An ethereal thing said inside his mind. He jumped, startled at this new symptom of insanity, and looked to make sure Dennis had seen. It had registered as more substantial and alien than an intrusive thought but not quite an auditory hallucination. Once again, it spoke voicelessly.

I didn't want to communicate in this way, but you are doing such a poor job. I really thought I'd re-assembled your neurological pathways better.

The 'Exalted One' just sat in silent horror at whatever was going on. He feared that if he showed any concern or evidence of his mental deterioration, his cover would be blown and this cult would discover his amnesia.

Just stay calm. I have speculated that if they find the truth about you, they will destroy you very quickly. I will assist where necessary but please stop forcing my hand. I have bigger things to focus on. You are in charge of keeping this ruse up for now.

The 'exalted one' turned his thoughts inward, hoping to communicate with this entity. At first, it was unsuccessful until he focused on the static and started his inner monologue.

"Umm, yeah, I figured as much. But what the fuck are you? What is going on."

A voiceless soundless entity isn't capable of sighing to express its pompous annoyance, But whatever it did, was the next closest thing.

To the best of your understanding, I am a being of coalesced sentient energy. I'm not getting into the specifics with you. We might be able to do that another time. Right now, the game is afoot. So you handle the humans, I'll handle the rest.

"The rest? What does that mean? What game?"

Respectfully just do as you told or I will disrupt your sinoatrial node and hop into that police officer and watch you flutter like a dying fish in this car. You are going to keep these people convinced that you are a powerful guru. Don't worry. I've made sure this should be an easy task.

"I don't know what any of this means"

That's the problem for all of this dreadful species just do what you're supposed to and stop wondering. Now, handle it.

And with that, the static shrank back, leaving the 'Exalted One' feeling quite lonely in the back of the cop car that was now driving down an even more dire looking street. The windows of buildings had been busted out, and many had black burn marks streaking out the empty windows. Yellow caution tape seemed to block these off, keeping people out for fear of structural integrity loss.

"We decided to move into the area's hit by the riots, authorities patrol them infrequently, and outsiders don't come here much. Gangs still make bases here and lurking out of here at night to slink around the city. Chief Collector Ahuja has decided we should reach out to them bring them into our fold, but many want only to lay low."

Dennis said.

The 'exalted one' nodded, contemplating the different implications before he spoke.

"We will have to wait the response of these gangs. Even in these times, it would be wrong to turn others away from the truth. But, if they will not see the truth, then we should not expend energy on such things."

He cleared his thoughts nervously after speaking, hoping that sounded like a statement an astute guru would say.

"Many will agree with you, Exalted One. It is so fortunate you have returned. The talk from the Collectors has been, well, apocalyptic at best. Many think they are gearing up for violence."

He did his best to stay stoic as he registered this.

"With my return, we shall become calm once more. It is important to keep our survival, and violence will only beget anger." Dennis, who just blew the brains out of his coworker a little over an hour prior, seemed to agree wholeheartedly with an eager nod.

"It is good to know everything will be okay." He said reassured.

The 'Exalted One' *tisked* at this follower.

"Now, now Dennis, we know nothing for certain. But no matter the outcome, we will have lived a life worthy of our Soul." He then wondered if maybe he'd been an actor before this. This was Grade A to improve work. He should be getting a check for it at this point, which brought up another good question. What was the median income of cult leaders these days?

The cop nodded and pondered over the words before speaking again, this time with grim determination.

"We shall. You are truly wise exalted one."

They rode down empty roads in silence for another ten or fifteen minutes before reaching a tall building that seemed to be a highrise hotel. Whatever logos it had near the entrance had been defaced and burned, and it looked like eight floors up a fire had broken out. It was taped off as some of the similarly damaged buildings were.

Dennis circled the building until he found the underground garage entrance attached to the seemingly deserted hotel. He spun to the bottom flow, parked the cop car in the farthest corner, helped the 'Exalted One' out of the rear seat, and advised him to step back from the car.

He then opened the trunk and fished out a small red jerry can that sloshed in his hand.

"What are you doing, Dennis?" the 'Exalted One' asked, apprehension heavy in his voice.

Dennis looked over at him.

"Each of these cars had a built-in GPS tracker. I already deactivated it but I need to be sure they can't manually turn it on after we are missing for too long." He said.

The cop began splashing gasoline over the front and back seats. The pungent chemical aroma lifted into the stale parking lot air. After the can was empty, he sat it inside the car over the computer, then took a few steps back and produced a zippo. With a flick of the striker, it sparked to life. He tossed the silver lighter into the front seat, and it roared to life and began sending acrid smoke out shortly. Dennis walked away from the growing arson case swiftly and softly grabbed the 'Exalted One's' arm, leading him away as well.

"Won't you get in some trouble for all this? It will be hard to hide Dennis." He asked.

Dennis closed his eyes, inhaled deeply, and exhaled before speaking with a voice close to cracking.

"This all is just another sacrifice I make for our collective soul."

"You are truly one of the best of us, Dennis." The 'Exalted One' said as they neared a set of scuffed metal double doors that looked to be some sort of workers' access to the hotel. Dennis rapped loudly on the doors, and shortly after, some shuffling could be heard on the other side. The doors opened a crack, and the head of a young Asian man with a rear-facing cap poked out.

His eyes switched between the pair, then back to the exalted one, and went wide with surprise.

"Get in quickly." He said in a hushed tone as he swung the door open.

The cop and the guru complied, hurrying through the door into the unadorned service hallway beyond. Once inside, the Asian man closed the door behind them and active some kind of lock with a definite *click*.

He turned and looked at the 'Exalted One' more time with added scrutiny.

"Is it really him?" he asked Dennis

"Truly." Was his simple reply.

Without hesitation, the man fell to the ground bowing as Dennis had in the park. The 'Exalted One' noticed that this man, too, had visible concentric geometric tattoos on the backs of his hands and knuckles. The 'Exalted One' knelt and helped the man to his feet and held the man's hands for a moment examining the tattoos in their familiarity spoke to some hidden meaning.

"I am one of the soldiers of the Soul Exalted one. My name is Casey."

"A true blessing!" The Exalted One said, clapping him on the shoulders and putting on a happy grin to mask the growing fear of whatever he was stumbling into.

"Exalted one." Came Dennis's grim voice from behind him.

"Yes, De...." He said, turning to see what he might need before being cut off by a terrible image. Dennis stood with a horrid look painted across his face. The kind of twisted frown and squinting eyes a child makes before balling that their parent is deserting them on the first day of daycare. Tears brimmed in the corners of his eyes like tipping cups ready to spill. In his right hand was the gun that had killed his partner, the man whose vest the Exalted one was still wearing. Only this time, he did not grip it as if to fire. Instead, he held it by the end with the grip towards Casey, who took it somberly into his hands before taking steady aim at Dennis's skull.

"When my body grows still, will you be the one to collect my soul?" as Dennis asked this, the tears ran down his square face.

"What is this!" the exalted one Demanded in a loss of his stoic composure. "What is going on?"

Dennis spoke up.

"With my partner dead and the car destroyed, only one loose end remains Exalted One. Suppose it is discovered or even believed that I have been aiding the Children of the universal Soul. In that case, they will dig deep into those I've been in contact with, and other agents of the collective will be found and brought down eventually; it may lead back here."

"Surely, there has to be another way? You've been so useful to us all, to me." He pleaded, but Dennis shook his head.

"No, Exalted One, I am sure of this. You must trust me."

"He is right. This has been a contingency for some time with our external agents." Casey said with a deadpan indifference.

"Chief Collector Ahuja and others agreed that it is better for them to end this way than have our work unravel. "

The Exalted one was about to open his mouth in protest once more when Dennis's tearful gaze locked with his own.

"I will be okay Exalted one. I would ask that it is you who collects my soul to return to the collection I would be honored."

The Exalted one nodded, unsure of what he'd even agreed to. Whatever it was, it brought a bittersweet smile to the young cops' face just before the pistol cracked, sending a hollow point bullet right between his eyes. Much like in the park earlier, a mess of thick gore flew from the now obliterated back of his skull. The concrete wall behind him was peppered with the thick concoction of bright blood and brains splattered in a runny Rorschach pattern. The ringing from the gunshot's proximity in the tight space meant that he couldn't hear the wet slap that had to have come with the splatter.

The morbid mix of iron and acetone denoting the stench of death, the overbearing ringing in his ears, and the subtle static in his mind, these were the sensations that prevented any attempt at the thought. He watched the dead man's arms twitch reflexively even while the brain had taken up residence on the far wall. He felt empty,

He *was empty.* Not even truly a man, he was nothing but an empty shell devoid of memory of the person he'd become. Someway, somehow, he felt that this was all his fault but, he couldn't even explain how he'd come to this fate.

Before he could further ponder his own culpability in all this, down the hall came to the *clack-clack* of heels on linoleum.

A middle-aged blonde woman in a long skirt and a blouse was stepping towards them with the determination that picked up when the exalted one came into her view.

"Exalted one!" she cried out as she neared them. Tears streamed down her face.

"I never thought I'd see you again!". She said, throwing her arms around his neck and hugging him. Whatever molecule of calm he had on reserve at this point fled him, and he was left struck by pure, unfiltered fucking panic that rattled the marrow from his bones. This woman had met him before. The gig was up. These freaks would skin him alive; they'd drink his blood while having a blasphemous orgy, they'd…they. The static flooded his mind once more. It was foggy, completely lacking any lucidity. A thought would begin to form and then turn intangible and slip away while he was left watching his body move, unable to discern what it was doing. He was speaking but knew not the words he said. The woman would respond. But she sounded far away, and her words inverted. At first, the state was distressing, but even that feeling slipped from him until there was nothing but the cold comfort of the static.

He came back. He was in full control but altogether in a state of confusion. The entity had taken over again. He must have been close to blowing their cover. He was annoyed by the dammed thing. It takes over his life, gets him into this mess, and they won't even tell him what's going on. Maybe this is all some fever dream. A delirium, and he's really a man dying in a hospital bed pumped such full meds.

All the signals that your nerves are perceiving are entirely concrete. Now listen before the game is lost. I do not have the energy to keep jumping into your messes.

Astounding, the voice in his head was chastising him.

"My mess? I have no clue what is happening! You're the mess maker. You've gotten people killed!"

You don't have the luxury of time for me to explain how you are wrong right now.

"Fuck you; you're least tell me your plan."

That would raise more questions from you, diverting attention from more important matters. I NEED energy and you are close to getting me some.

The static seeped down into his neck, nudging his head to turn and look once more at the dead body below them. Casey had set the gun aside and was removing the vest on Dennis's corpse. He then went to work unbutton his shirt and ripping away a plain white tank top to expose a single geometric tattoo positioned over the dead man's heart.

"Exalted one. He is ready for collection." He says before resting back on his haunches beside the body. The blonde woman stands a respectful distance away with an impassive look of reverence on her face.

His left hand moved, free of the statics guidance, pushed by muscle memory alone. It hovered over the tattoo until a warmth emanated accompanied by a soft glow like red candlelight. His open palm pressed down slowly until it was flush with the still-warm flesh underneath. The static sensation surged forth like a lightning strike down the limb. Instantly his hand felt held there by a magnetic force. His whole arm then shoulders were met by this creeping warmth. It moved up his neck until it flooded his mind causing the static to buzz pleasantly in his skull. With it came a natural, inviting calmness and easy euphoria. Below him, the flesh quickly was growing cold and blue. It seemed to shrivel and shrink against the frame of the bones. After about a minute of this, the body was ice cold and grey.

"He is with us once more." The exalted one said, moving his hand away with a lingering warmth clinging to his fingers.

A small pick me up but a needed one for what's to come.

"What is to come then?"

Not here, I instructed the woman behind you to bring you to a room where you may rest, and we may talk free of any...interlopers.

The 'Exalted One' felt numb, unsure of anything he didn't have any intent on arguing further.

"Ok"

"Casey dear, you can handle the rest of this, can't you." The woman said, shaking him free from his internal dialogue. "I will take you to your room at Exalted One."

Her name is Annice. She has been a follower since her husband died in a head-on collision. She met you when she was brought under Chief Collector Ahuja to be one of the collectors. You spoke very little due to the large following at the time, so don't overplay that you know too many details.

He didn't respond. He supposed the entity knew its message had been received. The 'Exalted One' rose and gave a waning smile to Casey. Before turning to Annice.

"Thank you, Sister. I have traveled far and been through much. I will need a night to rest and gather my thoughts before addressing the Children here."

She blinked behind the thin bifocals that gave her a librarian's visage and adopted a salesperson's thin-lipped smile as she spoke.

"I think the Chief Collector will want to speak with you tonight…" She said with the passive-aggressive of someone whose job might be on the line.

He held up a hand, his right hand, and her polite protests were silenced. The exalted one spoke

"The Chief Collector will wait. I have discovered the Lesser is coming towards this sanctuary, and I have come to its defense, but first, I must collect myself. tomorrow himself and any other leadership present will meet, and we shall form a plan of how we shall survive."   Annice nodded tersely before turning.

"This way, Exalted

one." And he

followed.

About 15 minutes later, he was looking at himself in the 5-star suites vanity mirror, seeing his full body for the first time in his accessible memory. A short, wiry man with little muscle on a thing frame but plenty of these damned geometric tattoos on every inch of his sun-dried skin. He might have been 30 something, but it was hard to tell as even on his sunken face and bald skull, the tattoos left inhuman patterns. All he had were pale almond eyes.

Do you like them? I pulled them from patterns created by examining the comatose portions of your mind.

"I don't know what they mean."

They don't mean anything. They are simply lines and dots.

"Then why are all these people covered in them?"

Through examining your memories, I discovered that humans perceive deep meaning in frivolous symbols and have built their information processing around them.

"Wait, do you mean language? Is this a language?"

No, it is just lines and dots. But your followers took to them fervently.

"*These aren't MY followers; I didn't even do this you did!*"

I took control, yes, but all of these tenants I pulled from your own creative processing and what you knew of other such organizations around the world.

"*Bullshit, I don't even know who I am. Why can't I remember anything?*"

I still keep a hold on your own mental capacity to maintain fluid control of this body. It senses part of that overlaps with your memories as specific neural pathways would allow you to contest me for custody.

"*What The FUCK, get out. Get out of my head!*"

He roared inside his own mind until he swore. He felt the static begin to ebb.

You possess great mental control. More than the majority of your species. It's something you had cultivated over years of some mental training. It made you a good host initially but as well meant that keeping your mind hampered has been a drain on my energy.

"*Is that why I am awake now? You got tired?*"

I do not tire but I am a being of pure energy. When I expand it, I am made lesser without a steady supply of energy to replace more of me. After creating an implosion to disrupt our attackers, we leaped through space and what you would understand to be time not long after I had to recoup lost energy, which I can do in only small parts from your own body.

"*But when you aren't feeding off me, what do you do? Do you always feed off the dead?*"

No, I can metabolize any source of Kinect, thermal, electrical, chemical, and even small amounts of light energy. But absorbing

the latent energy in living beings or their corpses impressed the
other humans and cemented their belief in your religion.

"My religion! What do you mean I didn't do this!"

He was disgusted at the implication. He may not have his memories,

But the disgust and fear of cult had been present since Dennis first pulled that trigger.

He walked away from the john doe in the mirror, turning toward the luxurious dark marble shower as he twisted the knob to let hot water flow over him. The entity pressed him with more information.

Yes, every bit of the belief and structure of it was pulled from the ideas and philosophies already present in your mind. The only interference I supplied was to ensure that I would be the victor in the game.

"What is this fucking game you keep talking about?"

There was a moment of mental silence before the static formed ideas once more.

I am in what you would consider a competition to see who can bring about the destruction of life in this world.

Even with water pouring hot over his skin, his blood ran cold with fear.

"What do you mean?"

I cannot express it much more directly. The Lesser and I are in a competition to end life in this world. We have been in the game for years in different ways. I have been winning; hence, I am the Greater, and it is the Lesser.

"You are trying to kill everything on earth! Why the hell are you doing that?"

It was merely the next agreed challenge. That Is all. I can see how this is distressing to you, and you will not like this, but you

do not have a say in this. If you try to resist, I will simply take over this body entirely again.

In a show of force, the static surged forth, nearly engulfing his mind, only this time, he did not sit by passively as it flooded about his skull. His mind fired back, and he centered himself with a single breath and exhaled. He found it had transformed into a mental wrestling match. He had to put one hand on the slick shower wall to keep him from collapsing. Terribly distorted memories slipped from the static to form lessons in stillness, of cultivating silent peace. *"You can't fight the lesser if you're fighting me the same time."*

The entity was enraged at this act of defiance. It turned from static to a blinding headache that sent needles through his brain and blacked out his vision. He fell to the shower floor and fought to rite himself into a cross-legged sitting position. Once there, he regulated his breathing focusing his efforts on the motion and its accompanying sensations until his heartbeat had begun to grow calm.

"You have overplayed your hand. You'd threatened to kill me and hop bodies earlier if I'd been non-compliant, but here, I am breathing. You need me. I'm not sure how or why, but you need ME."

The needles spread from his mind down his spin and out until his whole body was made into a pincushion. His breathing became ragged, but still, he kept it steady. His gut began heaving and his bowels and bladder failed him, but he still sat legs crossed, fighting to keep his focus on the breaths between bubbling bile that fought its way up his throat.

"I have nothing to lose."

He spat the thought angrily into the maw of fiery static in his mind, just before putting a bony fist through the glass sliding door of the shower.

"You do."

With blood-streaked hands, he gripped one of the pieces of shattered glass and began pressing it into his right side with just enough force to draw blood. If there was any pain, it was lost in the see of needles his body floated in.

"Without me, you lose; maybe you'll even die if you can."

He pushed a centimeter deeper ready to send his bowels pouring over the already desecrated marble floor of the shower, but then the pins disappeared, his stomach settled. The static in his mind fell back, cowed by his display.

Slowly, he let loose his grip and let the glass clatter to the floor. He leaned back out of breath, shaking but seemingly victorious.

"Now, you will tell me my name." A

moment passed. Then another, then

thoughts came.

Your name was Aran.

Aran closed his eyes and breathed a sigh of relief.

"Now, it is obvious we are tied together. We will work together for the time.
The rest of tonight, you will tell me as much as you can about You, Me, and The Lesser."

The static undulated in his mind like the wax in a lava lamp for a moment. It was weighing its options.

Very well.

The next morning The Exalted One awoke in the king-sized bed of

the suite to the sound of a polite knock at the door. They sat up, finding a soft bathrobe, and slipping into it before answering the door. Whoever had knocked no longer there, but they had left their suit now cleaned and pressed hanging on a wire hanger. On the front of the suit was pinned a note.

It read; *Chief Collector Ahuja has called a meeting at 9 am in the ground floor conference room. Your presence has been respectfully requested.*

His thoughts went back to what the greater entity had told him last night.

The Lesser is in this hotel. Of that, I am sure. I know not who he is occupying precisely as he can change hosts per the arrangement we had and leaps bodies often. I have my suspicions, though.

They put the suit on and steeled himself for what was to come. Then started a conversation with The Greater again

"Is your energy sufficient?"

Yes, considering the intermittence of the supply.

Before sleeping last night, The Greater had instructed him to tear the lamp wires' coating and wrap them around his fists while sleeping. He'd practically been charging it while he caught a few hours of sleep after their negotiations. He understood their game now and his part in it. The Greater had gotten boastful and said he could end this world using only one human. The Lesser saw this as an easy win and took the wager.

The walk to the conference room was silent both within his mind and without. Once they'd ridden the elevator down to the ground floor, it was easy to find. While most of the hotel they'd seen had been relatively intact, the rest of the lobby had been wrecked with whatever unrest had torn through this part of town. Bits of shattered glass from the ceiling height windows at the building's face littered the stained carpet floor. Furniture lay in smoldering ruin and scorch marks were scattered about like the impact site of a bombing run.

Yet, the front desk was intact. and behind it, he saw two more "Soldiers of the Soul." One young girl and one young boy These barely looked older than 15. Even one clutched a shotgun and the other an AR. They both bent their heads low respectfully as the

Exalted One strode past to the small faux-wood door with a large bronze placard over it reading CONFERENCE ROOM.

Their hand hovered over the door handle.

"Are you ready?"

Yes, are you prepared for the sacrifices that must happen."

"Yes."

With that, the weathered, tattoo strewn hand closed around the handle, turned, and pushed the door open.

It was a small room with bare white walls and a singular long lacquered desk made from a dark tree. Around its sides were over a dozen people of different ages and races, all covered in similar but distinctly unique tattoos. At the far end was Chief Collector Ahuja, a middle-aged man with a face of the stone. Dark both in complexion and demeanor with a grey speckled beard kept neatly trimmed with hair following suit. His tattoos grew out from his eyes, looking like angry, geometric cephalopods trying to engulf some deep see prey.

One empty chair was left at the opposite end of the oblong table.

The Lesser is in this room. I cannot discern with absolute certainty who it is inhabiting, but I stand by our assumption. Proceed with caution and follow the plan.

The collectors around the table's edge bowed respectfully to him and let out excited murmurings. Ahuja only lowered his head slightly in a deferential nod.

"I am truly touched to see you all!" The Exalted One proclaimed excitedly before sitting in the empty seat. They surveyed the hopeful faces as he spoke.

"Now, let us come together in these trying times to face our… true enemy."

Their gaze fixed on Ahuja at the end, whose stone still demeanor had not dropped.

Ahuja spoke his voice baritone and even-keeled.

"The Lesser." He said.

"Yes, he is here in the city." The Exalted one said. "Nearer than any of us could believe or would wish him to be." This revelation was met by a symphony of gasps and auspicious whispers.

Ahuja only smiled.

"Then you will agree with me that we should take a more... proactive approach to our defense with It and the governmental forces hunting us. We cannot simply wait around to be executed."

"Why doesn't he attack first? It's plain, he knows we are on to him, and all he has to do is destroy me to win.

I cannot say for sure. He may feel confident. The Synaptic energy footprint of the other collectors is more in line with his own. This means many are apt to trust him over you. In our absence, he has done quite a bit of politicking. They may be willing to come to his aide in open conflict, believing you to be now inhibiting the Lesser.

"And all of the collectors and soldiers have been altered to manipulate energy as I can haven't, they."

His thought brimmed with annoyance as he realized the position the greater had put him in. Being limited by this challenge to only one perishable person, it had manipulated some of the higher-level cult members' atomic makeup to imbue them with inhuman abilities. Thinking, if the Lesser attacked directly as his plans, he'd be annihilated by overwhelming force. It hadn't accounted for the more subdued approach the Lesser would take. Now that it had hijacked the cults fervor against them, the Exalted One was practically sitting in the lion's den.

"Then it's backed us into a corner, hasn't it."

Indeed, we must level the playing field.

The Exalted one took on a calm, knowing smile and outstretched their hands in an inviting, Christlike manner

"A change in our approach is most assuredly necessary, But First before we discuss our plans, let us join hands and align our souls so that will of the Collection shall be foremost in our decisions." The Collectors seemed to nod in agreement. Even if Ahuja/the Lesser had instilled doubt and shifted the paradigm of their beliefs, they still had enough respect to follow the traditions the Exalted One had put in place. The two nearest them grabbed their hands and slowly down the line. Each collector did likewise until the chain had extended all the way to Chief Collector Ahuja.

The Chief Collector hesitated a moment.

"Should we waste time on such frivolities. We are at war, are we not?" He asked the crowd of collectors, looked taken aback at the sacrilege. But the Exalted One let out a genuine laugh of good humor. Everyone in this room had heard it before. The laughter of a tutor teaching a well-meaning child who's strayed from the lecture.

"We are in a time of strife that is correct," they spoke, giving a gentle squeeze to the two at his left and right before continuing.

"We are assailed on all sides. From within and without, we face challenges and danger. These frivolities, as you called them, might seem like dead weight on a storm assailed ship. Things we may toss overboard to lighten our load easing our way home." His eyes canvased the rapt faces around him, and he spoke with enhanced vigor and more incredible determination as his words rolled on down their own warpath.

"But the coastlines are not our home, never have they been. We do not take to ports because we are not ships. We are more than vessels. We are the sea, and when storms grace our surface, we rise to the tumult, we rise and fall together knowing no hope of golden coast, instead of the certainty that we existed before such calamities and we shall exist after. These frivolities then cannot be dead weight. They are the disciplines that guide us until the storms pass. They are what sets us apart from the unguided energies that assail this world. "

The exalted one's words fell to a close on still faces that turned slowly to the only broken link in their chain. Ahuja started back nervously for a moment.

Prepare yourself.

But Ahuja simply took the hands to his left and right and locked eyes with the Exalted One.

"Your wisdom is truly *greater* than mine. My apologies." He said before kneeling reverently.

Now.

Energy surged forth with the eagerness of a breath long-held and flowed through the half dozen men or women to the Exalted One's right. They all immediately and in tandem contorted into twisted screaming visages robbed of any human dignity. Muscles and vessels bulged as they were pulled to their limits before snapping the bones beneath them. On their skin, the flesh pulled taught and colorless as if drained of their fluid. From their lungs came an orchestra of hollow squeals that could only be the sound of dying breaths passing through the vocal memories of the most excruciating pain a mortal mind can fathom.

For a single moment, a time hardly perceivable to anything that deems itself as thinking, the right side of that table was a line of howling corpses holding hands in a final sacrament. And after a single moment more, the left side became its horrid mirror.

But the Exalted one was ready for the return salvo, and as soon as it drew in the energy from the collectors on that side, it broke the chain on the left and sent a bolt of life through the cable of vice-like death grips on the right. The withered bodies on the right suddenly became a wave of convulsing bodies. As the energy shot through them, they swelled, the flesh bubbling on a subcutaneous level before bursting, each collector one after another in rapid concession went off like a fleshy string of Chinese firecrackers painting the interior of the room in fleshy strips and wet gore. When the bolt struck Ahuja, his body went flying back smoldering as it burst through the wall he'd been facing and out into the street beyond. Overhead, the lights flickered in an epileptic fit.

The Exalted One lunged past the corpses in a single inhuman leap. His right arm covered in seemingly forgotten blisters and burns with strips of burned suit trailing as he swept across the room. He leaned against the hole and peered out into the light of day that filtered back through it.

Lifting itself already was the disjointed, bent body of Ahuja, still clad in its black salwar suit, like a horrid marionette whose lines had been twisted. The left side was scarred with deep tissue burns exposing frayed threads of sinew pulling at blackened cracked bones. It leaped to the left, clearing the site of impact and the view afforded by the hole in the wall in a single movement.

A dissonant voice called out through what was left of Ahuja's Larynx in a taunting tone.

"I didn't think you'd kill your playthings so quickly!"

It does not know you have cognitive control. Do not let it.

Before Aran could speculate if that advice were of self-preservation or preservation of its pride, a blur of movement caught his eye just above him. The horrid corpse puppet had scaled the sider of the building like a spider and was attacking downward with bits of energy crackling like a thousand sparklers along with the blackened claw that swiped at his head. The Exalted One tilted their head back just as the attack passed, then reached up, gripping it at the wrist.

264

Pulling down, the Lesser was thrown onto the bits of the broken wall the body had just passed through moments ago.

The Exalted One roared at the corpse, all heavenly tones fleeing their voice.

"You shouldn't have dirtied them then!"

The body was impaled through its core by a mess of tangled rebar and exposed metal, but still, it lurched too. Face blank and entirely devoid of life, yet words still gurgled forth from its gaping mouth.

"Either you're holding back," an invisible wave of force erupted between the two forms sending the Exalted One flying through several floors of the hotel before cratering the roof of a vacant suite and falling to its carpeted floor in a broken hump. Rising through the hole was the twisted form of the Lesser.

"Or, you are still very weak after our last scrap." It crawled across the floor towards the limp form of the Exalted One. When it was near enough, it loomed over the other. Its head lulled limply to one side, the eyes a flurry of spasms under half-open lids.

"No matter." It said, "Both of these are close to death, which means you'll have lost soon."

The Exalted One shot a hand out, hooking the thumb into the side of Ahuja's neck. A ripping blast tore what flesh was left, severing the head from the meat in a smoking flash. The broken body fell in a dead heap atop him.

Pain tore through the Exalted One. Bones were surely splintered, and organs were ruptured. They tried to push the corpse of them but was met with only more unanswering limbs and a fresh wave of pain. Aran wanted to scream out at the invalidity that had been laid upon them but found his mouth silenced.

Static.

It had replaced the pain.

We do not have time for that. The lesser will be back shortly. It only needs moments to find another host, but we have at least destroyed the most dangerous one. I can repair some of the damage to keep us moving.

Aran slipped back as the greater flooded deeper, turning his attention to the broken body of the Exalted One.

"It was right. You have lost. This body won't last."

I can repair it. I can recuperate, I can…

"YOU have lost."

The Lesser flexed its energy across the neurons of this new host. It was youthful and without damage, one of the "Soul's soldiers. Not quite so mentally proficient as the Chief Collector had been, but the little religion The Greater had fostered was a perfect environment for cultivating reasonable minds for their inhabitation. These soldiers were especially useful as some of them had already had the molecular structure changed to be used as weapons when the proper energies were applied. It was much more efficient than plucking a random creature that would get torn to pieces by such use. A pubescent voice sounded to his right

"Gordan? Are you okay?"

The Lesser turned the host to look at the body it had already perceived before the eyes could view it. It was one of the other soldiers, a significantly younger one, a thin female. For a fraction of a second, it sifted through the shattered memories of the host and found this little creature's name. Jenna. The host's right hand grabbed the top of her head and drained all of her in a flash. The pale body turned to a shriveled, wailing mummy that crumbled to ash in its grasp before a scream could even be uttered. Dead silence pervaded the lobby. It wasn't limited to any human perception its host had.

266

It perceived the two dozen other soldiers of the Soul in the lobby. It could hear their stifled gasps. It could listen to the disgusting undulations inside the ventricles in their heart as they pumped blood in a furious panic. It could even hear the gasses effusing in their lungs. Pitiful things The Greater had finally fallen to hubris with this last wager. It would be The Lesser if it kept up such nearsightedness. Hungrily, he felt the vibrations put off by the rapid firing of the nerve clusters around their little hearts and the flurry inside all their organic minds. It had been reserving itself since taking on the guise of the Chief Collector to keep station. Its host began leaping from human to human tearing their bodies to pieces while it tore into every bit of energy. He could shred them molecule by molecule in blinding flashes. Until the only form standing was its host, left enveloped by blood, bone, and carbon residue. It slunk towards the elevator finding the 15th-floor button and pressing it that was where he'd left them. When the doors open, it still stepped with caution. Whatever was left of the Greater's little experiment might always be able to put up a fight, and he wanted this game to be over already. Finally, it came to the door that held the greatest energy signature—leveling the right hand against it. No chances this time.

The Lesser let lose a concussive blast so strong it turned the host's arm into a smoldering stump and everything beyond that into ruin. Floors of the hotel were turned to debris that tore through the neighboring buildings like a shotgun blast. The host stood inches from the gaping wound The Lesser had created in the side of the building. It scanned the grey cloud and space beyond for the energy signature. Excitement rippled when it picked it up. Down there in the street.

It sent the host plummeting the fifteen stories down to the street. It's entire lower body would have crumpled immediately, but The Lesser stitched the bones back with lightning speed enough to keep it standing so that it could saunter forth, legs bowed, cracking and creaking with each step. It knew it didn't matter. This host had nearly run its course. The Greater was there just barley its signature was so faint now, but it found it. It was clinging pathetically to the nearly destroyed form of its'

267

host, *The Exalted One,* which the others had called. The frail thing was laid overtop apiece of rubble like a sacrifice upon an altar. It had no lower body and its dust-covered entrails hung loose in the debris, blood, and brain spilled forth from a cavitated skull like strewn meat. Whatever was left of this human had seconds left on its life.

It bent over the desecrated body.

Are we about finished yet? There's little of you left. Don't die with this human out of pride.

It was shocking when the body croaked the response.

"Not yet."

The right hand shot up and, from its palm, a massive explosion blossomed, tearing through matter until it began splitting atoms in a blind fury. It was leveling the entire city in a final act of defiance.

The Lesser was ejected from the instantly obliterated host, terrified by the show of force. It rose from the planet, lapping up the energy of the nuclear blast hungrily growing and growing, all the while thinking of what it could do with such a body of energy at its disposal. Surely it would soon be of sufficient strength to engulf stars again. Maybe after this defeat, The Greater would be tired of terrestrial things, and they could take the game to new heights. Where was The Greater? It hadn't had much energy left, and that parting blow would've taken most of it. Had it committed some kind of megalomanic suicide? The Lesser began surveying the planet and everything in orbit, looking for its partner and without, and it might have nearly missed it. The signature was small, made both diminutive and strange by the injury, leaving it a fledgling thing barley itself.

The Lesser reached out. It had no desire to look for a new partner to play with and did not wish to take on the dreary solitary solemnness others of their kind had pursued. Instead, it reached out and began transferring bits of energy to its competitor in an attempt to save its sentience from deteriorating any further. The meager thing could barely hold itself together.

Well, I hope you've learned something.

The Lesser stated as it nursed The Greater, but no thought was given back, only a staunch cerebral silence.

Come now, you still have two victories. Let us get our strength back and move on from this place. The nuclear stockpiles and the core should do us well.

Still, only empty silence as more and more energy was drawn away.

Fine, we will call it a draw. You were handicapped in this bout and plenty of life still yet exists. We will split it down the middle.

The silence pervaded intolerably and the Lesser grew annoyed with this infantile behavior. It had never seen the Greater act in such away. It tried to retract its flow of energy but found it couldn't. The other was feasting on it and wouldn't let up.

What is the matter with you? Have you forgotten how to act in defeat?

The silence was broken by a hollow thought unrefined and unrealized. Even worse, it was disturbingly unfamiliar in its mannerisms.

"Defeat?"

It asked gravely. The Lesser tried to retract once again but the hunger was reaping energy off it, and The Others essence was penetrating it. The Greater was still attacking!

Please stop this! This is ridiculous. Stop this, you lost!

The Greater's presence had become parasitic feasting on it in a panic. It tried to fight back but found that it had grown weaker and weaker as the other overtook it.

"Lost? I have only begun to play your game."

The final scraps of sentience were being shredded along with the energy it rode but enough remained yet for the Lesser to experience a dreaded revelation.

You aren't the Greater. Who are you? The Lesser was already too weakened to perceive the answer when it came. Only the hollow expanse of the void was left to hear the echoless proclamation.

"I am The Exalted."

About the author-

Robert T. West is an active-duty navy Corpsman who has spent the peak of his military "career" attached to the peacetime USMC infantry. He lives wherever the government currently decides he should or in his horrifying conversion van that hopefully will never end up in your city but inevitably will.

@writingsfrom_a_deadworld

Art- @jesse_martin

Cover Design- @midnight.oil.design

www.ingramcontent.com/pod-product-compliance
Lightning Source LLC
Chambersburg PA
CBHW030820090426
42737CB00009B/809